W9-BSI-787

Claudio Rodríguez and the Language of Poetic Vision

Claudio Rodríguez and the Language of Poetic Vision

Jonathan Mayhew

Lewisburg
Bucknell University Press
London and Toronto: Associated University Presses

Associated University Presses
440 Forsgate Drive
Cranbury, NJ 08512

Associated University Presses
25 Sicilian Avenue
London WC1A 2QH, England

Associated University Presses
P.O. Box 488, Port Credit
Mississauga, Ontario
Canada L5G 4M2

The paper used in this publication meets the requirements
of the American National Standard for Permanence of Paper
for Printed Library Materials Z39.48-1984.

Library of Congress Cataloging-in-Publication Data

Mayhew, Jonathan, 1960–
    Claudio Rodríguez and the language of poetic vision / Jonathan
Mayhew.
        p.   cm.
    Includes bibliographical references.
    ISBN 0-8387-5174-1 (alk. paper)
    1. Rodríguez, Claudio—Criticism and interpretation.   I. Title.
PQ6633.034Z78   1990
861'.64—dc20   89-42931
                                                                     CIP

PRINTED IN THE UNITED STATES OF AMERICA

La poesía es una aventura lingüística
[Poetry is a linguistic adventure]

—Claudio Rodríguez

Contents

Preface

The self-reflexivity of modern poetry has led critics to an increasing fascination with the poet's own aesthetic ideas. *Poetics,* originally literary theory in general, has come to refer as well to the theoretical consciousness that underlies the writing of poetry: a modern poet must not only write poems, but also develop a rationale for what he or she is attempting to accomplish. For many twentieth-century poets the creative and the theoretical aspects of poetry cannot be separated: poetics is no longer an assortment of opinions about the art of poetry, expressed in prose, but a rigorous, coherent, and self-conscious exploration of the possibilities of language, carried out in the poetic medium itself.

The present study is an attempt to elucidate the poetry and poetics of Claudio Rodríguez, one of the most notable voices in contemporary Spanish literature. For Rodríguez, born in Zamora in 1934, poetry is essentially language. He has declared, "En la poesía la palabra no es un vehiculo: es la creación del poema. No es un medio expresivo. La palabra *funda* el poema" [in poetry the word is not a vehicle: it is the creation of the poem. It is not an expressive medium. The word founds the poem].[1] In contrast to the more explicit linguistic self-consciousness of much contemporary Spanish poetry, however, Rodríguez's work comments upon itself in an oblique, metaphorical manner: language or poetry per se is rarely its stated subject. His few prose statements, moreoever, emphasize the irrationality inherent in the art of artistic creation. As an "inspired" poet, who claims not to exercise fully conscious control over his work, Rodríguez appears to stand at the opposite pole from the cerebral, Mallarméan writer. Unlike some of his contemporaries, he has avoided the temptation to theorize at length. Most of his comments about his own work are vague and evasive, directing the reader back to the poetry itself: "El pensamiento poético," he has asserted, "nunca es explícito; está implícito en la creación" [Poetic thought is never explicit; it is implicit in creation].[2]

The emphasis on poetics so frequent in contemporary crit-

icism often leads to a privileging of metapoetry in its most obvious manifestations. Rodríguez's reticence, in contrast, has
allowed many critics and readers to overlook the self-reflexive
dimension of his work almost completely. Taking their cues from
the poet's own apparent distrust of theory, they have underesti-
mated his awareness of the problems of poetic language. The
advantage of Rodríguez's indirect approach to these problems,
however, is that it makes poetics and poetry, theory and practice,
virtually one activity. His meditation on language is less overt
than that of other poets, but by the same measure it gains in
subtlety. Inconspicuous to the casual reader, it can only be
brought to light through a careful scrutiny of the text.

   Rodríguez's implicit mode of self-consciousness has another
important consequence: not only is his poetic thought embodied
in the poetry itself, but his vision of language is an integral part of
his vision of the world: the same vision of the sign underlies both
his linguistic self-consciousness and his engagement with reality. His meditation on language is not merely one concern among
others, then, but a coherent structure that gives shape to his
work. My focus on Rodríguez's linguistic self-consciousness is
not reductive; it does not aim to exclude any other of the important themes of his work: the natural world, social solidarity, or
love. It could be argued, rather, that such a focus provides the
most *inclusive* view of his poetic thought, illuminating not only
Rodríguez's vision of language, but also the way in which this
vision informs other, seemingly unrelated facets of his poetry.

   The semiotic consciousness of modern poetry can be defined
in terms of the opposition between two contradictory yet interdependent ideas: a belief in the motivation of the linguistic sign,
and the opposing attempt to create an arbitrary and therefore
autonomous poetic language. The first chapter of this study, "The
Language of Poetic Vision," explores this opposition in theoretical terms. Rodríguez is notable not only for the complexity
of his semiotic thought, but also for his awareness of the ethical
dimensions of poetics language. In this respect he is part of a
larger movement of younger poets such as José Angel Valente and
Jaime Gil de Biedma, who react against the more limited poetic
theory of the older "social poets."

   Rodríguez shows an awareness of the problems of poetic language from the very beginning of his career. At the same time, his
work moves through a series of distinct phases. The main body of
my study follows the development of Rodríguez's poetic thought

through close readings of each of his four published volumes of poetry, *Don de la ebriedad* (Gift of drunkenness, 1953), *Conjuros* (Incantations, 1958), *Alianza y condena* (Alliance and condemnation, 1965), and *El vuelo de la celebración* (The flight of celebration, 1976), as well as of poems not yet collected in book form.

The first of Rodríguez's works, discussed in chapter 2, "The Crisis of Visionary Poetics in *Don de la ebriedad*," is in many respects the most remarkable. Written and published when its author was still a teenager, this sequence of fragments is an allegory of poetic vision that bears little or no relation to the political and existential tendencies that dominate Spanish poetry in the 1950s. Each of Rodríguez's books is structured around an opposition between two conceptions of poetic language. In *Don* this opposition is formulated in terms of a conflict between a transcendent poetic vision, in which the poet seeks to escape time, and a more authentic poetics of participation. The following chapter, "The Motive for Metaphor: *Conjuros* and the Rhetoric of Social Solidarity," reveals the fundamental problem inherent in the poet's participation in the life of his times: the loss of critical distance. *Conjuros* can be read as Rodríguez's response to a common question in postwar Spanish poetry: that of the poet's place in society. Whereas *Don de la ebriedad* demonstrates the difficulty of a detached, alienated vision of reality, Rodríguez's second book reverses this process, revealing the problems involved in the attempt to participate in the historical world through language.

Chapter 4, "*Alianza y Condena*: The Dialectic of the Sign," is a reading of Rodríguez's most explicitly metapoetic work, his most systematic exploration of the duplicity of language. This collection takes up the theoretical problem suggested in *Conjuros* and reframes it in more explicitly semiotic terms, as a conflict between the motivation and the arbitrariness of the sign. *Alianza y condena* thus represents a breakthrough in Rodríguez's development as a self-conscious manipulator of metalanguage.

In my readings of Rodríguez's first three books I stress the incompatability of the two opposing attitudes toward the sign. My penultimate chapter, "The Language of Paradox and the Paradox of Language: The Later Poetry," deals with the poet's attempts, in his later poems, to fuse the two opposing impulses that shape his work into a single, paradoxical language, one that both affirms its unity with the world and reveals its own arbitrary nature. Claudio Rodríguez's work, a sustained and coherent meditation on language, exemplifies the rigorous self-consciousness of modern poetry. His poetics reflects the struggle to come to terms with the two equally crucial but essentially contradictory attitudes toward the sign. My concluding chapter, "Modern Poetry and the Language of Criticism," addresses two of the central concerns of the study as a whole: the inseparability of the two theories of poetic language, and the relation between literary self-reflexivity and the language of criticism. Many recent critics have claimed that self-conscious literature involves the reader more actively in the creation of meaning. The poet in Rodríguez's work is essentially an *interpreter* who depends upon his own language to make sense of the phenomenal world. The critic, in turn, is placed in the position of interpreting the poet's interpretive acts. As he or she is caught up in the hermeneutical strategies within the text, the act of reading, like that of writing, becomes a self-conscious exploration of the problems of signification.

I was introduced to Claudio Rodríguez's poetry in a class given at the University of Madrid in 1979 by the poet himself. I am indebted to him for his poetry as well as for his help in the spring of 1985, when he agreed to talk with me once again about his work. Several other individuals have aided me in bringing this study to its completion. Andrew P. Debicki offered early encouragement and advice, and later offered invaluable suggestions for improving the completed manuscript. I have also benefited from the close readings of Michael Predmore, Alban K. Forcione, and Madeline Sutherland, who have helped to guide this project from its inception. My greatest debt, finally, is to Akiko Tsuchiya, who for the last seven years has been my closest companion as well as the ideal reader of my work.

Claudio Rodríguez
and the Language
of Poetic Vision

1
The Language of Poetic Vision

The poet thinks with his poem.
>—William Carlos Williams

One of the central features of literature since the Symbolist movement is its self-conscious reflection on the possibilities of its own language. Roland Barthes has described Stéphane Mallarmé's "heroic will to identify, in one and the same written matter, literature and the theory of literature."[1] In the past one hundred years this identification has ceased to be heroic: it has become virtually routine. The tendency that in recent years has become known as postmodernism posits as a fundamental axiom the inseparability of theory and practice, exaggerating the self-consciousness that is already explicit in the work of many of Mallarme's modernist heirs.[2]

The identification between the theory and practice of literature has significant implications or critics of twentieth-century writers. If poetic language is already a commentary on itself, then it is no longer possible or even desirable to treat it merely as the *object* of critical discourse. In order to interpret the poem, one must first take into account the poem's own interpretation of itself and ultimately come to terms with the theory of language implicitly or explicitly articulated in the poet's work. As Barthes has suggested, the critic's task is to "decipher the literary word not as the dictionary explicates it, but as the writer constructs it."[3] This imperative, it should be emphasized, is not valid exclusively for modernist or postmodernist writers. One lesson that these writers teach is that virtually all literature reflects upon itself at some level. Recent critics have been exploring the self-consciousness of writers of all epochs, not merely that of obvious precursors of modernity such as Sterne and Cervantes.

The self-reflexivity of modern literature spans literary genres and national boundaries; it is evident in the plays of Pirandello, the novels of Flann O'Brien and Miguel de Unamuno, and the

15

poetry of Wallace Stevens and John Ashbery. In the immediate context of modern Spanish poetry, Claudio Rodríguez is heir to a rich tradition of self-consciousness. Theoretical reflection is already a crucial element in the postsymbolist verse of Juan Ramón Jiménez, one of the dominant figures of Spanish poetry before the civil war. Poets of the 1920s, especially Pedro Salinas and Vicente Aleixandre, wrote with an increasing awareness of the problems of poetic language. Although the poetry of the immediate postwar period is still often seen in terms of its religious, existential, and political themes, I would argue that self-reflexivity is an important element in most of the noteworthy poets of this period. A case in point is the poetry of Blas de Otero, the most significant poet of the politically committed "social poets." The generational group of the 1950s, which includes Claudio Rodríguez, José Angel Valente, Angel González, and Francisco Brines, along with novelists such as Juan and Luis Goytisolo, represents an explosion of self-consciousness in contemporary Spanish letters. Poets and novelists younger than Rodríguez have continued this trend, so that both metapoetry and metafiction are now well established in Spain.

The self-consciousness of modern poetry is often the result of a conflict between two opposing yet interdependent notions of poetic language. Gerald Bruns has succinctly defined these ideas as "hermetic" and "Orphic":

> We can call the first idea "hermetic" because the direction of the poet's activity is toward the literary work as such, that is, the work as a self-contained linguistic structure. . . . We can call the second "Orphic" after Orpheus, the primordial singer whose sphere of activity is governed by a mythical unity of word and being, and whose power extends beyond the formalism of a work toward the creation of the world.[4]

One's first impulse might be to attempt a classification of modern poets and writers according to their implicit theory of language: Beckett, for instance, would be "hermetic," while Rilke would be "Orphic." The difficulty with such a categorization, however, is that the two attitudes toward language are more often than not inextricably intertwined in the work of a single writer. The modern poet's attitude toward the word is essentially contradictory. Mallarmé, the prototype for the hermetic writer, also saw poetry as an "Orphic explanation of the Earth." Jacqueline Brogan has studied the poetry of Wallace Stevens in terms of a conflict between "logocentric" and deconstructive notions of language.[5]

It would be a mistake, then, to explain away one dimension of such a poet's work in an effort to achieve consistency. Bruns himself stresses the interdependence of Orphic and hermetic poetics: it is not a question of classifying poets into discrete and opposing categories but rather of exploring the complex inter-relations between two equally crucial ideas of poetic language.

The poetry of Claudio Rodríguez, like that of Mallarmé and Stevens, reflects the contradictions inherent in modern poetics. These contradictions have produced divergent critical responses to the work of the Spanish poet. For the majority of critics the author of *Don de la ebriedad* is an Orphic poet, an essentially innocent creator whose words directly reflect an unmediated communion with the natural world. Dionisio Cañas's phenomenological approach to the poet is one of the best developed articulations of this perspective, which is also implicit in the criticism of several other Spanish critics.[6] At the other end of the critical spectrum, a few North American hispanists have identified his poetics with the poststructuralist critique of representation. Martha LaFollette Miller defines Rodríguez's poetics in terms of his "linguistic skepticism," the distrust of language that is the characteristic mark of modern writers such as Samuel Beckett.[7] Andrew Debicki and Margaret Persin have studied the way in which his style often subverts the "message" that the speaker is ostensibly communicating, thus setting in motion a deconstructive play.[8]

The critic's vision of Rodríguez's poetic language will depend to a large extent on the theory of the sign already implicit in his or her approach. Generally speaking, thematic paraphrases of Rodríguez's poetry tend to stress the link between language and the world, while stylistic analyses reveal the arbitrary and indeterminate nature of his language. While several critics have discerned both Rodríguez's Orphic faith in the word and the arbitrariness of his language, no critic to date has explicitly come to terms with the potential contradiction between these two aspects of Rodríguez's poetics. A complete view of his thought must not only recognize the two opposing impulses toward the sign but also account for their dialectical interaction.

The Orphic theory of poetry, is based, as Bruns points out, on "the mythical unity of word and being." In semiotic terms this unity can be expressed in terms of "Cratylism," or the belief in the motivation of the sign.[9] (This doctrine takes its name from Plato's dialogue "Cratylus," in which a character of the same name argues that names directly imitate the things they represent.) Contrary to Ferdinand de Saussure's contention that the link between the signifier and the signified is arbitrary and conventional, this theory holds that the sound of the word is motivated by its meaning. The implications of Cratylism go far beyond the more obvious phenomena of onomatopoeia or sound-symbolism. For Gérard Genette, the belief in the motivated sign is "the implicit fundamental article of our literary aesthetic."[10] This article of faith is evident in the commonplace notion that literary language is richer in meaning and more expressive than ordinary discourse. Any appeal to the indissolubility of form and content, sound and sense, language and meaning, implies that the writer aims to close the gap between the signifier and the signified, to use words as naturally motivated signs, while the critic's fundamental task is to discover the intimate correspondences between the thematic and formal elements of the text.

Several other theorists have emphasized the centrality of the Cratylist ideal. E. L. Epstein, for example, views stylistic mimesis as the most important criterion of literary value in post-Renaissance European literature. He claims that we no longer value formal patterns for their own sake (as in medieval Welsh poetry) but demand that these patterns be correlated with the semantic features of the text.[11] Several of the major structuralist theorists, similarly, have questioned the relevance of Saussure's doctrine of the arbitrariness of the sign to the study of literature. Barthes asks (rhetorically) whether it is possible to be a writer at all without believing in "the natural link between names and essences."[12] Tzvetan Todorov, similarly, takes Saussure to task for his blindness to symbolic thinking.[13]

The rival theory of the literary sign stresses the arbitrariness of language, the distance between reality and its representation. Whereas the first theory emphasizes the expressive power of language, the second envisions language as an autonomous system to be valued for its very distance from reality. Although it stands Cratylism on its head, this second, formalist theory of literary language does not reject its fundamental premise: that language has meaning insofar as it imitates the world. Its implicit argument is that if language is not mimetic, it cannot be meaningful at all. It is not merely that words are conventional tokens but that their conventionality actually impedes them from communicating meaning or from referring to reality. It is in this sense that this poetic idea of arbitrariness is distinct from Saussure's theory. For Saussure the arbitrariness of the sign does not impede the functioning of language. Quite to the contrary, it is only through linguistic conventions that we are able to communicate at all. For the poet, on the other hand, the arbitrariness of language severs it from the world, making it a radically autonomous, "hermetic" form of discourse.

The modern poet does not choose between motivation and arbitrariness but rather strives to construct a language that is at once expressive and autonomous. From one point of view this paradox is only apparent, for it is resolved in the literary work itself. Both functions of the sign, after all, are inherent in the literary use of language and coexist in the same words. The problem of language in modern poetics, however, results from the underlying contradiction between these two visions of the sign. Not only does one vision exalt the autonomy of the signifier, while the other sees the signifier as a reflection of the signified, but each defines itself in opposition to a negative version of the other.

The Cratylist ideal of natural language seeks to remedy the arbitrary meaninglessness of conventional discourse. Genette has distinguished "primary Cratylism," the naive belief that language is already naturally motivated, from "secondary Cratylism," the effort to compensate for the inadequate motivation of a language that one recognizes to be merely conventional.[14] It is this second version that is predominant in modern poetry after Mallarmé. Few poets would claim that words, as they already exist in everyday usage, magically correspond to something beyond themselves. The poet's task, rather, is to transform the arbitrary and therefore impoverished signs of ordinary language into the motivated signs of poetry. As Barthes suggests, the writer subverts language only in order to rescue it once again.

> In literature, particularly, any subversion of language is identified contradictorily with an exaltation of language, for to oppose language by means of language is always a claim to liberate a "second" language which is then the profound, "abnormal" (protected from norms) energy of utterance; hence the destructions of language often have something sumptuous about them.[15]

If Cratylism stands opposed to the straw man of a discourse governed by conventional norms and therefore emptied of its meaning, the opposing ideal of literary autonomy seeks to avoid a language that is, in a sense, too meaningful: the deliberately arbitrary signs of poetry free language from an unimaginative copying of reality. Each idea of poetic language, in short, can have either a positive or a negative value. Motivation represents either the power of language to give meaning to the world, or the tyranny of referentiality. The arbitrariness of the sign, in contrast, represents (positively) the free play of the signifier, or else (negatively) the emptiness of conventional language. Such arbitrary language is either autonomous, freeing us from the practical demands of a utilitarian language, or else it is deceptive, in which case it masks the true nature of things and alienates us from the world.

Definitions of poetic or literary language have often striven to differentiate it from ordinary language. The contradictory functions of poetic language, however, mean that this opposition will be highly ambiguous. Genette has observed that Roman Jakobson formulates the opposition between ordinary and poetic language in two contradictory ways. On the one hand a mimetic poetic language stands opposed to a conventional prose; on the other hand an autonomous poetic language contrasts with a mimetic referential language.[16] Is poetry, then, more or less mimetic, more or less autonomous, than nonliterary speech? It is clear that the most significant opposition in this case is between two dimensions of the sign—mimesis and autonomy—rather than between two fundamentally different kinds of discourse. While neither dimension belongs exclusively to poetic language, it is poetry that most clearly dramatizes their contradictions.[17]

Efforts to define poetry have usually pointed to the more obvious formal qualities that distinguish it from prose. An exclusively formalist approach, nevertheless, leaves unanswered the question of the ultimate *function* of poetic language. To affirm that poetic language is language used for its own sake rather than for utilitarian ends still does not give us a clear picture of what this autotelic language would strive to be. In other words, such an affirmation begs the question of what language is in the first place. The same formal means that would appear to make language more mimetic also increases its autonomy. To imitate the world is also to attempt to replace it: the most powerfully mimetic signs would become things in their own right rather than merely representations of other things. The attempt to heighten the expressive capabilities of language, then, inevitably involves a focus on language for its own sake. Meter and rhythm provide the clearest examples of this paradox, for to write in verse is simultaneously to create the illusion of a more directly expressive language and to manipulate the purely formal qualities of language as an autonomous system, and thus shift the attention of the reader away from the meaning being expressed. A similar analysis would apply to figurative language. Even if the sound of a word is arbitrary, a figure of speech can be a motivated sign: Samuel Taylor Coleridge distinguishes the arbitrary "allegory" from the motivated "symbol." The sound of rose bears no relation to the idea, yet the idea of a "rose" is a natural sign of beauty or passion. Metaphors, all the same, can also be viewed as essentially artificial devices that emphasize the distance between poetry and reality. The rose, my example of a "natural sign," is, after all, the most conventional of symbols. The endeavor to create a more natural language, whether through versification or figurative language, has the effect of making language more artificial, arbitrary, and autonomous.

Up until this point I have been considering poetic language in terms of its relation to the world, as either a mimesis of reality or as a subversion of this mimesis. The problem with this schema, however, is that it assumes that reality itself exists independently of language. For a poet such as Claudio Rodríguez, on the other hand, the world itself has a specifically linguistic structure. The words of the poem refer not to a reality that exists anterior to the word but rather to another system of signs, which one could call the language of poetic vision. As Octavio Paz writes, "Todo lo que nombramos ingresa en el círculo del lenguaje y, en consecuencia, a la significación. El mundo es un orbe de significados, un lenguaje" [All that we name enters into the circle of language and, consequently, into signification. The world is an orb of signifieds, a language].[18] The relation of poetic language to the world, then, is the relation of one system of signs to another. If poetic language is the interpretation of the signs of the world, the poet's theory of language will imply a vision of reality as well. What might at first appear to be a reductive move, a radical denial of the existence of anything outside of language, leads to a more inclusive vision of language as a means of engaging with the world. Many critics have stressed Rodríguez's concern for human life in all its dimensions. This humanism, however, is based on a semiotic insight: "Indeed, it is the realization that the whole of human experience, without exception, is an interpretive structure mediated and sustained by sign, that is at the heart of semiotics."[19] The Orphic ideal of poetic language takes nature as its model. The signs of nature are transparent, signifying through their direct link to the reality they represent. The language of the poem will strive to attain the condition of these natural signs by overcoming the mediation implicit in the linguistic sign. The hermetic theory of poetic language starts with the opposite premise, that the signs of nature are themselves inherently opaque and arbitrary. Things are not what they seem to be: surface appearances form a veil which conceals the truth. Rather than attempting to model language after nature, this theory takes the duplicity of human speech as a model for understanding the phenomenal world itself. If the language of reality is itself duplicitous, then the ideal poetic language will no longer imitate this language but rather unmask it. The function of poetic language is paradoxical, for it is its arbitrariness that gives the poet the power to see beyond the arbitrary signs of the world and thus to reveal the truth.

The relation of poetic language to the signs of the world is not only an aesthetic problem but a moral one as well: both the Cratylist idea of a natural language and the opposing notion of the capacity of language to unmask illusions have clearly ethical implications. These implications are perhaps implicit in all theories of poetic language. In the context of postwar Spanish poetry, however, they become an overriding preoccupation. The poets of Rodríguez's "generation," who begin to write in the 1950s, are explicitly concerned with developing an ethics of the sign. They are preoccupied with what Barthes, around the same time, termed "the morality of form."[20] In contrast to the dominant voices of the time, the "social poets," who tend to oppose their own political commitment to any aesthetic concern at all, these younger poets emphasize the ethics of aesthetics itself. "Art for art's sake" or "pure poetry," and its apparent opposite, the neglect of style in the name of content, are fundamentally similar in that they both assume that the medium of language is *irresponsible*. In other words, both tendencies divorce aesthetics from social concerns. It is interesting in this respect that José Angel Valente, the most articulate spokesman of the young poets of the fifties, accuses the older social poets of an inverted version of the formalism they claim to oppose: "Por vías distintas, el antiformalismo ha venido a parar en un formalismo de la peor especie: el de los temas o el de las tendencias" [By different routes, antiformalism has come to rest in a formalism of the worst type: that of themes or tendencies].[21] Rodríguez, in a strikingly similar comment, equates these two extremes: "La poesía como noticia . . . puede compararse con *el arte por el arte*. Funciona en otra dirección pero se asienta, en el fondo, en los mismos postulados y fines decadentes" [Poetry as news . . . can be compared with art-for-art's sake. It works in another direction but it rests, at bottom, on the same decadent postulates and ends.][22] "Formalism," in other words, implies the severing of form from content, language from meaning. Seen from this perspective, the ideological clichés of the social poets are as empty of true significance as are the decadent verses of the fin de siècle.

For the younger poets of Rodríguez's time, the social function of the poet is not to express a particular political message but to transform the sign itself. José Angel Valente entitled his book of critical essays "Las palabras de la tribu," alluding to Mallarmé's well-known idea that the poet's task is "to purify the language of the tribe" ["*donner un sens plus pure aux mots de la tribu*"]. Valente does not interpret Mallarmé's line as a call to rarefy poetic language, to convert it into a "pure" speech far removed from the everyday. Rather, he sees the poet as one who cleanses language of its corruption. In this view the poet becomes at once the destroyer of the conventional codes of social discourse and political ideology, and the creator of a new and more authentic speech. A frequent motif in the poetry of the period is the empty sign, the word that has lost its capacity to signify. In many poems of Rodríguez, Valente, Angel González, Gloria Fuertes, and others, the more authentic speech of poetry stands opposed to this meaningless, conventional system of tokens.

The main problem with this opposition is that there is a potential contradiction between the critique of the sign and the attempt to "make it new." Language can be false in two distinct senses: first, because it is used to lie in particular instances (propaganda, official discourse, cliché), and second, because it is *inherently* deceitful, never coinciding completely with the truth. Umberto Eco pointedly defines semiotics as "*the discipline that studies things which can be used to lie.*"[23] In this second, more profound sense, any truly authentic language will be illusory. The destruction of language characteristic of modern poetry is an attempt to liberate a second language, but this new poetic language will be potentially false in that it will be a system of signs. Since the poet's own liberated speech will be vulnerable to the same critique, the cycle of the destruction and re-creation of language can never come to an end.

Rodríguez is acutely aware of the essential duplicity of poetic language. He tends to avoid the simple opposition between the meaningful and the empty sign, or between poetic and conventional language, found in the work of some of his contemporaries. Instead, he struggles with the opposition between the motivation and the arbitrariness that is inherent in the poetic sign itself. His work alternates between two opposing and interdependent impulses. In the first of these, the poet identifies the motivation of the sign with his own union with the world, attempting to integrate himself into the world through a "natural" poetic language that corresponds directly to the signs of nature itself. His own language must become identical to the language of nature, in which appearances correspond directly to reality, the sign to the referent. Rodríguez has defined poetry as a form of *participation*: "Nace de una participación que el poeta establece entre las cosas y su experiencia poética de ellas, a través del lenguaje" [It is born of a participation that the poet establishes between things and his poetic experience of them, by means of language].[24] It is language that serves to mediate between the objective ("las cosas") and the subjective ("su experiencia poética de ellas"). The poet's participation, however, involves a blindness to this potentially duplicitous mediation, and thus a kind of self-deception. In spite of his reliance on linguistic mediation, he strives to participate in the world in an immediate way, as if this language did not exist.

The other main impulse in Rodríguez's work is to stand apart from the world in order to attain a more critical vision of reality. In this case the poet recognizes and even welcomes the duplicity of language, for it is this duplicity that allows him to question false appearances. Instead of condemning language as a deceptive imitation of nature, he conceives of nature itself as a shadowy world of illusory signs. His own words, in contrast, becomes a means for revealing the truth that these signs conceal. The inherent falseness of language makes it ideally suited to the task of exposing the falseness of other signs. If the danger of direct participation in the world is self-deception, the critical vision of reality easily leads to alienation. Each of the two impulses, like the two visions of language on which they are based, constitutes a critique of the other. By immersing himself in reality, the poet loses his capacity to discern the truth; detaching himself once again, he loses his connection to the world. The conflicting demands of language make it impossible for him to choose between these two alternatives. As I shall attempt to demonstrate through my readings of Rodríguez's poetry, the development of his poetic thought reflects the constant struggle to reconcile the two opposing theories of the sign and the two ethical postures they imply.

2
The Crisis of Visionary Poetics
in *Don de la ebriedad*

Quelle déception, devant la perversité conférant à *nuit*
comme à *jour*, contradictoirement, des timbres obscur ici, là
clair.

What disappointment, faced with the perversity that confers
to the word *nuit* [night] as to *jour* [day], contradictorily dark
tones to the latter and bright to the former.

—Mallarmé

In 1953, at the height of the vogue for social poetry, a student still
in his teens created a minor sensation in the Spanish literary
scene by winning the "Adonais" prize for *Don de la ebriedad*
(Gift of drunkenness), a short sequence of poems whose exploration of the problems of poetic vision seemed to bear little or no
relation whatever to the poetry of postwar Spain. Claudio
Rodríguez would soon become one of the best-known poets of his
generation; the poems of *Don de la ebriedad* would eventually
pass into many anthologies. Yet the fame Rodríguez's early work
attracted was never matched by careful critical attention. At the
time *Don* originally appeared it was treated as a brilliant anom-
aly, the product of a gifted but immature author. Rodríguez began
to receive serious criticism only after the publication of his third
volume, *Alianza y condena*, in 1965. By this time a number of
other younger poets had established their reputations:
Rodríguez's work could now be read in the context of an entire
poetic generation's reaction against the political preoccupation of
the earlier postwar poets. As Rodríguez's reputation has grown,
each new work has received more attention than the previous
one. In the process, however, the earlier works have been ne-
glected. This is doubly unfortunate: not only does *Don de la
ebriedad* contain some of Rodríguez's most brilliant poetry, but it
is in this book that his poetic thought takes shape. The conflict

between the poetics of transcendent vision and the poetics of participation contains within it all the elements that define Rodríguez's subsequent poetics.

Perhaps one need look no further than the book's title in order to locate a more profound source of the critical neglect of this book. Drunkenness is a traditional representation of the irresponsibility of poetic genius. The Platonic notion of the divinely inspired and therefore dangerously irrational nature of poetic creation implies that the poet is not really conscious of what he is writing. In critical comments about Rodríguez's early work the idea of unconscious genius is firmly linked to the poet's youth and supposed immaturity. This is not a premise that leads to careful analysis: if the poet is not fully aware of what he is writing, why should the critic treat the work seriously? It seems far better to stand back in admiring silence. This laudatory but distant approach can be convenient as well, given the extreme difficulty of many of the poems in *Don de la ebriedad*. To be fair, it must be noted that Spanish critics of the 1950s would have lacked the critical tools to undertake a detailed analysis of such a work. The notion that a poem could be a meditation on its own linguistic nature was not common critical currency at the time.

Yet the *topos* of drunkenness has other implications for the study of Rodríguez's earliest poetry. It can suggest unconsciousness, but also heightened consciousness. In fact, it is the contradictory nature of the state of inebriation that is most significant here. On the one hand, drunkenness involves the breaking down of the boundary of between self and other. Octavio Paz argues that wine is the social drug par excellence: "Circulación de la esencia vital, su acción entre los hombres es semejante a la del riego en la agricultura. Además, es el transmisor de la simpatía: exalta, comunica, reúne." [Circulation of a vital essence, its action among men is similar to that of irrigation in agriculture. In addition, it is the transmitter of sympathy: it exalts, communicates, unites.][1] Irrigation, not coincidentally, is one of Rodríguez's preferred metaphors in *Don de la ebriedad* and subsequent works. His poetry often seeks the exaltation of communion, in the sacramental sense, with both nature and humanity. At the same time, alcohol can be profoundly alienating, creating a barrier between the self and the outside world. The drunk is both gregarious and suspicious, open to the world and closed within himself.

Rather than assigning to the "ebriedad" of the title a single, univocal meaning, then, we should see it as a cluster of contradictions. The "gift of drunkenness" is at once a state of poetic inspiration, beyond the conscious control of the poet, and a manifestation of extreme poetic self-consciousness. As I shall argue in this chapter, there are two main conceptions of poetry at work in these poems: a timeless poetics of alienated vision and a participatory poetics that involves a surrender of the self. The poet-protagonist of this book views the poetic act in a profoundly divided state of consciousness.

The central event in *Don de la ebriedad* is the arrival of dawn. Almost every poem in the book presents some version of this event. The poet envisions the transition from night to day as a process of unveiling: the darkness opens up to reveal the light that has been implicitly present all along. Dawn thus represents the culmination of the poet's vision, the fulfillment of his desire. He is able to sense the presence of the light while it is still imprisoned within the night, and, through the revelation of poetic language, he is able to anticipate its imminent arrival. The coming event will confirm this predawn vision, realize it in the world. An eternal state of potential dawn, of light in tension with darkness, will take form as an event in time. A transcendent poetic language that allows the poet to see beyond deceptive appearances will become immanent in the landscape. The word will be made flesh.

Dawn appears as the culminating moment of poetic vision, then, but also as the *reversal* of this vision, the point at which it is transformed into its diametrical opposite. Even as it fulfills the predawn prophecy, it makes the prophet and his language unnecessary. The literal light of day displaces the metaphorical illumination of poetic creation. The most privileged moment for the poet actually precedes daybreak rather than coinciding with it. The event itself brings about a crisis of interpretation in which the poet can trust neither his previous vision nor his newly awakened senses. To resolve this crisis he must ultimately accept the loss of his privileged position. Before dawn, language represents the possibility of unmasking deceptive appearances, of revealing the light hidden within the darkness. It can do so only because of its inevitable distance from reality, its incapacity to coincide with what it names.[2] The actual unveiling of the light marks the end of this ideal of poetic language. At this point the gap between language and the world takes on a negative value: nature itself becomes the more genuine language, and the poet's human language becomes an obstacle to his communion with the world. In several powerful poems he calls for a sacrifice of his own language, identified with his alienated self, so that he may become an integrated part of a larger whole.

In order to understand *Don* as a metapoetic text, then, one must first perceive the central parallel between *language* and *vision*. The poet's predawn, visionary consciousness is defined primarily by its linguistic nature. More specifically, it results from an awareness of the arbitrariness of the linguistic sign, and of the distance between language and reality. Of course, in strictly semiotic terms the arbitrariness of language does not necessarily lead to a state of alienation from the world. For the poet, however, language is the only means of access to reality. Thus the integration of oneself into a larger whole becomes inseparable from the task of overcoming the duplicity of language.

As a book of poems, *Don de la ebriedad* consists of a series of disjunctions. Light emerges from darkness and, simultaneously, displaces the poet's previous vision of the dawn itself. The complex interpretive crisis that results from this displacement is "resolved," finally, in an appeal to a natural simplicity. These transformations are so radical that they threaten any coherent reading of this sequence of nineteen closely interrelated poems. The ground shifts under the reader's feet as each new stage in the story changes the way in which the preceding one is to be understood. To reach the end of the story, the point at which the transformation from a visionary to a participatory poetics is complete, the poet, and the reader along with him, must deny the steps that led up to it. These steps, in other words, lead toward their own destruction.

A more practical difficulty is that of reconstructing a narrative order in the first instance, for the organization of the poems as a sequence is not self-evident. Rodríguez coincides with his critics in calling *Don* a single long poem rather than a collection of shorter ones: ". . . se trata de un solo poema, dividido arbitraria-mente en fragmentos" [It consists of a single poem, arbitrarily divided into fragments] (16). These fragments invite the reader to organize them into a larger whole. At the same time the poems, as the author has arranged them in book-form, follow neither a well-defined narrative sequence nor the chronological order in which they were written.[3] Rather than depicting single moments in the story of the dawn, individual poems offer different, at times contradictory, versions of the same event. No one clear sequence of events emerges, for the stages in the progression overlap. In order to make sense of *Don* the reader must create a new order out of the fragments, although the disjunctiveness of the work means that no one definitive order can exist.

Any analysis of the problems of reading *Don* presupposes a prior interpretation of the text. The first step of the argument will be to decipher the central patterns of imagery in *Don*, to trace the process by which the predawn light of poetic vision emerges from the darkness and takes form in the world, simultaneously destroying itself. From there I shall attempt to unravel the poet's ambivalent response to this event. By resisting his own displacement, he remains with an interpretive crisis, an endlessly repeating cycle of anticipation, revelation, and disillusionment. In order to accept his destiny, on the other hand, he must submerge himself, rhetorically, in the natural cycle of life and death. The question of the reader's response to the poet's dilemma will lead back, once again, to the problems of making sense of the radical disjunctions of *Don de la ebriedad*.

No single poem embodies the privileged moment right before dawn, when light is still concealed within the darkness in its pure form. The poem that best illustrates the idea of the "eternal dawn, when light is still concealed within the darkness, in its event. The predawn vision appears as a response to this crisis, a retrospective glance at a moment that has already passed and perhaps never existed. The double status of the dawn—as eternal state and temporal event—makes it peculiarly elusive. The poem begins with the paradox of an extremely rapid unveiling of an unchanging situation:

> Yo me pregunto a veces si la noche
> se cierra al mundo para abrirse, o si algo
> la abre tan de repente que nosotros
> no llegamos a su alba, al alba al raso
> que no desaparece porque nadie
> la crea, ni la luna, ni el sol claro.
>
> $(1^{\circ}$ II, 34$)^{4}$

> I wonder at times if the night
> closes itself to the world in order to open, or if something
> opens it so suddenly that we
> do not reach its dawn, dawn in the open air
> that does not disappear because no one
> creates it, neither the moon, nor the bright sun.

The simple opening and closing of the night suggested in the first two lines quickly gives way to a more complicated version of dawn. The speed of the event puts it out of reach. Yet it was present all along. Belonging to neither night nor day, the product of a third, unexplainable force, it appears suddenly, although it has never actually disappeared. The gap between the eternal state and its realization in time makes it impossible for the poet to coincide with the privileged moment of revelation: he comes too late or too soon, never at the exact instant when time and time-lessness intersect.

Having missed the dawn, the poet returns to the moment right before, when the light is still only implicit within the darkness. He laments his inability to see the light *before* it is actually revealed in the dawn:

> Mi tristeza tampoco llega a verla [el alba]
> tal como es, quedándose en los astros
> cuando en ellos el día es manifiesto,
> y no revela que en la noche hay campos
> de intensa amanecida apresurada,
> no en germen, en luz plena, en albos pájaros.

> Nor is my sadness able to see it [the dawn]
> just as it is, remaining in the stars
> when day is manifest in them,
> and it does not reveal that in the night there are fields
> of intense, hurried daybreak,
> not in seed, in full light, in dawn-white birds.

Kenneth Burke has pointed out that there is no negative for the imagination: a poet cannot negate an image in the reader's mind.[5] The nonrevelation of the light here ("*no revela*") has the force of an affirmation, as often occurs in the long, negative sentences in the poetry of Vicente Aleixandre. (Note also the indicative mood: one would expect the subjunctive "haya" after "no revela.") The last line of this passage totally reverses the tentative beginning of the sentence by appearing to deny the unrealized quality of the concealed light: "*no en germen, en luz plena, en albos pájaros.*" Rodríguez's negation of his own vision shows its essentially *linguistic* character. Burke notes that there is no negative in nature, only in language: "*The essential distinction between the verbal and the nonverbal is in the fact that language adds the peculiar possibility of the negative.*"[6] Rodríguez's entire conception of night, as the absence or negation of light, rests on the assumption that the world itself is a system of signs. The night is a deceptive mask. Rodríguez's aim, as Joaquín González Muela asserts, is to unveil the truth, "ver la realidad desenmascarada de su falsa apariencia" [to see reality unmasked of its false appearance].[7] The metapoetic character of Rodríguez's dawn is also evident in the extreme suddenness of the event. In nature the coming of the day is a more gradual process, while in the poems of *Don de la ebriedad* it is envisioned as an instantaneous unveiling of hidden light.

The privileged moment of vision, ambivalently negated and affirmed, precedes the dawn itself. The poet values the hidden light for its very inaccessibility to the senses. It represents the implicit and the potential in opposition to the explicit and the already realized. The ideal revelation of the light is indirect, either distant in space or postponed in time. The visionary poet, by attempting to go beyond the world, places himself in a position of maximum risk:

> ¿Qué puedo hacer sino seguir poniendo
> mi vida a mil lanzadas del espacio?
> Y es que en la noche hay siempre un fuego oculto,
> un resplandor aéreo, un día vano
> para nuestros sentidos, que gravitan
> hacia arriba y no ven ni oyen abajo.

> What can I do except continue to place
> my life at a thousand lance-blows of space?
> And it is because in the night there is a hidden fire,
> an aerial brilliance, a day in vain
> for our senses, that gravitate
> upwards and do not see or hear below.

This affirmation of the concealed light confirms the "nonrevelation" earlier in the poem. The final lines of the poem present the idea of an eternal dawn.

> Así yo estoy sintiendo que las sombras
> abren su luz, la abren, la abren tanto,
> que la mañana surge sin principio
> ni fin, eterna ya desde el ocaso.

> Thus I am feeling that the shadows
> open their light, open it, open it so much,
> that morning rises without beginning
> or end, eternal already from the sunset.

The "eternal" vision in *Don de la ebriedad* is paradoxical. It is at once timeless and temporally conditioned, a state without beginning or end, and the result of a particular event. It both anticipates and follows the dawn. The poet privileges, alternately, the potential, concealed force of the moment before sunrise and the splendor of the revelation itself. Another poem, which could be read as a direct continuation of "Yo me pregunto a veces," establishes a direct correspondence between the light and the poet's desire, a force that seeks fulfillment, but also, ultimately, its own destruction:

> Así el deseo. Como el alba, clara
> desde la cima y cuando se detiene
> tocando con sus luces lo concreto
> recién oscura, aunque instantáneamente.
> Después abre ruidosos palomares
> y ya es un día más. ¡Oh las rehenes
> palomas de la noche conteniendo
> sus impulsos altísimos! Y siempre
> como el deseo, como mi deseo.
>
> (1º IV, 36)

> Thus desire. Like the dawn, clear
> from its height and when it stops
> touching with its light the particular
> newly dark, although instantaneously.
> Then it opens noisy dovecoats
> and it is already one more day. Oh the hostage
> doves of night containing
> their highest impulses. And always
> like desire, like my desire.

The image of the doves being released from their dark cage is another version of the "albos pájaros" of the light-within-darkness. In this poem the tension between light and its dark covering becomes even more acute. The poet attempts to describe the moment between night and day, the instant in which the light is still concealed but yet is already being revealed. The eternal, unrealized dawn struggles to break out of its dormant state. As a figure of desire, the predawn light is inherently unstable: its essence, like that of desire, is to become something other than itself. It finds fulfillment in the world, transforming itself into the colors of the morning landscape:

> Vedle surgir entre las nubes, vedle
> sin ocupar espacio deslumbrarme.

No está en mi, está en el mundo, está ahí enfrente.
Necesita vivir entre las cosas.
Ser añil en los cerros y de un verde
prematuro en los valles . . .

See it surge up between the clouds, see it
without occupying space dazzle me.
It is not in me, it is in the world, it is there before us.
It needs to live among things.
To be indigo in the ridges and a premature
green in the valleys. . . .

A central metaphor in *Don de la ebriedad* is that of the seed, the exemplification of the potential, the latent, the unseen. The light germinates in darkness and flowers at dawn:

> Ante todo,
> como en la vaina el grano, permanece
> calentando su albor enardécido
> para después manifestarlo en breve
> más hermoso y radiante . . .

> Above all,
> like grain in its sheath, it stays
> warming its burning dawn-whiteness
> so as then to make it manifest in brief
> more beautiful and radiant . . .

The final lines of the poem lead up to the moment of consummation, when desire is finally incarnated in the world:

> Mientras, queda
> limpio sin una brisa que lo aviente,
> limpio deseo cada vez más mío,
> cada vez menos vuestro, hasta que llegue
> por fin a ser mi sangre y mi tarea,
> corpóreo como el sol cuando amanece.

> Meanwhile, it stays
> clean without a breeze to scatter it,
> a clean desire more and more mine,
> less and less yours, until in the end
> it is able to become my blood and my task,
> corporeal as the sun when it dawns.

Since the light corresponds explicitly to the poet's desire, the sunrise is a moment of personal triumph. The identification here is so close that it would be possible to read the poem as if it were spoken by the personified sunlight itself. The incarnation of the day, when the verbal light is made flesh, is also the moment in which the poet/sun gains a physical body. In one sense this moment is the culmination of visionary poetics: through his privileged language, the poet has created his own self and his own world. (He remains the alienated subject whose vision depends on his transcendence of ordinary perception.)[8] The incarnation of the light, however, also marks the beginning of a transition from a visionary poetics to a poetics of participation. As soon as the poet's vision becomes corporeal, it also becomes vulnerable to death. The next step after the incarnation is the sacrifice of the flesh, in which the poet seeks to lose his individual body once again so that he may participate in the natural world (form a part of it) without the mediation of language.

The reversal of vision is instantaneous. Once the revelation has been completed—consummated and consumed—the poet has no more function in the world. The poem that stands at the head of *Don de la ebriedad* (in this case the position of the poem is significant) presents the entire cycle of the dawn, from the pre-dawn vision to the final moment of sacrifice, as a single movement:

> Siempre la claridad viene del cielo;
> es un don: no se halla entre las cosas
> sino muy por encima, y las ocupa
> haciendo de ello vida y labor propias.

$$(1º\ I,\ 33)$$

> Always the clarity comes from the sky;
> it is a gift: it is not found among things
> but much above, and it occupies them
> making of it its own life and work.

The paradox here—the light stands above things, not among them, but occupies them—is the result of the juxtaposition in a single sentence of two consecutive moments. The light, at first disembodied, almost immediately takes form:

> Así amanece el día; así la noche
> cierra el gran aposento de sus sombras.
> Y esto es un don. ¿Quién hace menos creados
> cada vez a los seres? ¿Qué alta bóveda
> los contiene en su amor?

> Thus the day dawns; thus the night
> closes the great chamber of its shadows.
> And this is a gift. Who makes the beings
> less and less created? What high chamber
> contains them in its love?

Because the darkness contains the light, nightfall and daybreak are parallel and reversible movements. The arrival of the darkness is the closing of the shadows around a potential dawn ("se cierra al mundo para abirirse"). Night uncreates the world in order to make possible a second creation; it gives by taking away:

> ¡Si ya nos llega,
> y es pronto aún, ya llega a la redonda,
> a la manera de los vuelos tuyos
> y se cierne, y se aleja y, aún remota,
> nada hay tan claro como sus impulsos!

> Why, it is already reaching us,
> and it is still early, it is already arriving roundabout
> in the manner of your flights
> and it circles, goes away and, still remote,
> there is nothing as distant as its impulses!

In this passage the night is seen as the potential day. The absence of a stated subject and the strange doubling of the light   who or what is the second-person singular of "los vuelos tuyos"?—increases this ambiguity.[9] The arrival of night/day is simultaneously the promise of a gift and the threat of a destruction:

> Oh, claridad sedienta de una forma,
> de una materia para deslumbrarla
> quemándose a sí mismo al cumplir su obra.
> Como yo, como todo lo que espera.
> Si tú la luz te la has llevado toda
> ¿cómo voy a esperar nada del alba?
> Y, sin embargo—esto es un don—mi boca
> espera, y mi alma espera, y tú me esperas,
> ebria persecución, claridad sola
> mortal como el abrazo de las hoces
> pero abrazo hasta el fin que nunca afloja.

> Oh, clarity thirsty for a form,
> for a matter to bedazzle
> burning itself as it fulfills its work.

Like myself, like everything that waits.
If you have taken away all the light
how can I hope for anything from the dawn?
And, nonetheless—this is a gift—my mouth
waits, and my soul waits, and you await me,
drunken persecution, clarity alone
mortal like the embrace of the scythes
but an embrace that until the end never loosens.

The clarity—light, brightness, transparency—is a disembodied desire that seeks an object in which to take form and simultaneously destroy itself. Just as night made possible a new beginning by "making things less and less created," the dawn will destroy them again through its re-creation: it will take away the light in the act of giving it. At the end of this lyric the poet waits for the dawn not as the fulfillment of his desire for an eternal, transcendent vision, but rather as the ultimate end of this desire. While night represents the germination of the light, dawn is an almost simultaneous flowering and reaping. As an event in time the dawn thrusts upon the poet an awareness of his own mortality, of the impossibility of preserving his alienated, visionary self.

"Siempre la claridad viene del cielo" is a microcosm of *Don de la ebriedad*: it distills the transition from implicit night to exlicit day that is the central event of the sequence. What is missing from this representative poem is the crisis that results from the poet's resistance to his loss of vision, to his new status as victim. Other poems in the book, to which I now turn, offer more difficult and more disjunctive versions of the same cycle. The final sacrifice of the self is implicit from the very beginning, but *Don* is the story of the poet's struggle to resist this sacrifice for as long as possible, to preserve his own ego beyond the initial moment of revelation and reversal.

Dawn, traditionally, is a moment of origin, of absolute beginning. Dionisio Cañas's essay on Rodríguez, "La mirada auroral," emphasizes the positive connotations of the event: "Es . . . su mirada poética, su lenguaje, un saludo feliz a lo auroral del hombre y del mundo" [His poetic gaze, his language, is a happy salute to what is dawn-like in man and in the world].[10] For this critic, the darker side of Rodríguez's vision is but a temporary abberation, a passing cloud that only confirms an essential enthusiasm for life. The dawn that appears in the poems of *Don de la ebriedad*, however, is the very moment when the "auroral" vision reaches its crisis. It is a point of disjunction in which the light of day displaces the poet's precarious predawn revelation. Even the poems that best illustrate the poetics of vision must be understood, ultimately, as reactions to a *loss* of vision.

It is significant that the first poems in *Don de la ebriedad* that Rodríguez composed, most of them contained in the third section of the book, are those that most directly reflect the poet's disorientation. The sequence begins, in this sense, as a response to the crisis rather than as an affirmation of the supposedly "original" vision. Dawn is already the moment after: it brings a nostalgia for the (hypothetical) originary moment before the unveiling of the light:

> Lo que antes era exacto ahora no encuentra
> su sitio, no lo encuentra y es de día,
> y va volado como desde lejos
> el manantial, que suena a luz perdida.

(3º I, 55)

> What before was exact now does not find
> its place, it does not find it and it is day,
> and the source, sounding of lost light,
> goes flying off as if from a distance

The day, then, represents the dislocation or displacement rather than the culmination of poetic creation. It calls into question the predawn vision of perfection, so that one cannot even be sure that any such privileged moment ever existed:

> No es que se me haya ido: nunca ha estado.
> Pero buscar y no reconocerlo,
> y no alumbrarlo en un futuro vivo. . . .

(3º VI, 61)

> It is not that it has left me: it has never been.
> But to search and not to recognize it,
> and not to illuminate it in a live future. . . .

What the poet has lost is not the thing itself but the expectation of attaining it in an imminent but always deferred future. Poetic vision in *Don de la ebriedad* can exist only as an anticipation of a coming revelation, never as an event in the present. The future

will be a single, unified moment in which the poet can coincide
with his creation. The present, in contrast, is inherently divided
against itself. The multiplicity of the newly awakened world
immediately raises the problem of interpretation. While the night
was the false covering of the light, the unveiling of day does not,
as might be expected, reveal a single image of the truth. Rather,
the poet witnesses a cyclical pattern of images that destroy themselves as they take form:

> Las imágenes, una que las centra
> en planetaria rotación, se borran
> y suben a un lugar por sus impulsos
> donde al surgir de nuevo toman forma.
> Por eso no sé cuales son éstas.
> Yo pregunto qué sol, qué brote de hoja
> llegan a la verdad, si está más próxima
> la rama del nogal que la del olmo,
> más la nube azulada que la roja.

(1º VI, 37)[11]

> The images, one that centers them
> in planetary rotation, are erased,
> and rise by their impulses to a place
> where, surging up again, they take form.
> Thus I do not know which ones these are.
> I ask what sun, what sprouting of a leaf
> reaches the truth, if the walnut branch
> is closer than that of the elm,
> the blue cloud closer than the red.

He must learn to distinguish the truth from its apparently identical double image. The opening lines of the first poem that
Rodríguez wrote pose a similar dilemma: "¡Qué diferencia de
emoción existe / entre el surco derecho y el izquierdo, / entre esa
rama baja y esa alta!" (3º VII, 62) [What difference of emotion
exists / between the right furrow and the left, / between that low
branch and that high one]. Such an exclamation must also be
read as an interrogation: what is the difference between two
parallel furrows or two branches? How can the poet discriminate
between the wealth of images that arise with the unveiling of the
light?

> Quizá pueblo de llamas, las imágenes
> encienden doble cuerpo en doble sombra.
> Quizá algún día se hagan una y baste.

(1º IV, 38)

Perhaps a people of flames, the images
light a double body in a double shadow.
Perhaps one day they will become one and it will be enough.

Each image is doubled, and then quadrupled, since each has a
shadow as well. (A single, unified image, once again, can only
exist at some moment in a hypothetical past or future.) The poet's
efforts to sort the true from the false image soon become too
much for him: he cannot keep pace with the rapidly accelerating
cycle of creation, destruction, and re-creation. As a part of this
cycle himself, he is as vulnerable to replacement, to death, as are
the images he evokes. As in the final lines of "Siempre la claridad
viene del cielo," he becomes a sacrificial victim. In contrast to
the more definite, controlled tone of this poem's conclusion—
"mortal como el abrazo de las hoces / pero abrazo hasta el fin que
nunca afloja"—poem VI, of book 1 seems to spin out of control at
the end. The poet is still caught up in the interpretive doubt that
comes with the arrival of poetic drunkenness:

> Aunque el alcohol eléctrico del rayo,
> aunque el mes que hace nido y no se posa,
> aunque el otoño, sí, aunque los relentes
> de humedad blanca . . . Vienes por tu sola
> calle de imagen, a pesar de ir sobre
> no sé qué creador, qué paz remota . . .

(1º VI, 38)

> Although the electric alcohol of the ray,
> although Autumn, yes, although the dews
> of white dampness . . . You come by your sole
> street of image, in spite of going on
> I don't know what creator, what remote peace . . .

The lyric poet uses language in an attempt to arrest time. By
interpreting the darkness linguistically, as the deceptive sign for
the light, the poet of Don aims to create an eternal, static version
of the dawn. The eternal dawn is unstable, however, to the extent
that language is a primarily *temporal* medium that inevitably
subverts any desire to escape from time. The process of unveiling, in which the light of day emerges from the darkness, is
identical to the unfolding of a sentence in time. Like the light,
poetic language consumes itself in the act of revelation. In constant movement itself, it cannot immobilize or contain the truth.
The poems of crisis, in Stanley Fish's phrase, are "self-consuming artifacts." More even than Fish's seventeenth-century texts,

they subvert their own meaning in the process of reading. A typical sentence describes the circular movement of revelation by employing a circular pattern of syntax:

> La belleza anterior a toda forma
> nos va haciendo a su misma semejanza.
>
> (3ºVII, 62)

> Beauty prior to all form
> goes about making us in its own semblance.

The paradox here results from the temporal flow of a language that attempts to capture the event *as it occurs*. The beauty has no form of itself, yet (as it takes form) it makes the world over in its own image. Here is a more extreme example:

> Nadie ve aquí, y palpitan las llamadas
> y es necesario que se saque de ello
> la forma, para que otra vez se forme
> como en la lucha con su giro el viento.
> Como en la lucha con su giro. . . .
>
> (3º VI, 61)

> No one sees here, and the calls palpitate
> and it is necessary to take the form
> out of this, so that once again it can be formed
> like the wind in its struggle with its gyrations.
> As in its struggle with its gyrations. . . .

These circular patterns have a dizzying effect on the reader. Like the poet, whose perception of the world is an act of linguistic interpretation, the reader of the text must make sense of a cycle of signs that appear to destroy themselves in the act of taking form.

The goal of the poems of crisis, then, is to prolong poetic vision beyond the problematic moment of its origin by means of a language that, like the vision itself, is ambiguously eternal and temporal. Since the revelation involves the instantaneous displacement of vision, the attempt to preserve it takes the form of repetitions which are, necessarily, derivative shadows of the "original" moment. Each morning must be a new beginning:

> (Sigue marzo)

> Todo es nuevo quizá para nosotros.
> El sol claroluciente, el sol de puesta,

muere; el que sale es más brillante
cada vez, es distinto, es otra nueva
forma de luz, de creación sentida.
Así cada mañana es la primera.
Para que la vivamos tú y yo solos
nada es igual ni se repite. Aquella
curva, de almendros florecidos suave,
¿tenía flor ayer? El ave aquella,
¿no vuela acaso en más abiertos círculos?
Después de haber nevado el cielo encuentra
resplandores que antes eran nubes.

(3º II, 57)

    Everything is new perhaps for us.
The bright-shining sun, the setting sun,
dies; that which comes out is more and more
brilliant, it is different, it is a new
form of light, of felt creation.
Thus each morning is the first.
So that we live it, you and I alone,
nothing is the same nor repeats itself. That curve,
sweet with the flowering almond trees,
was it in flower yesterday? That bird,
does it not fly perhaps in more open circles?
After having snowed the sky finds
radiances that before were clouds.

The absolute originality of the new day is a fiction, qualified from
the very beginning: everything is new *perhaps*. Instead of "*this*
morning is the first," the poet writes "*each* morning": each repetition, that is to say, attempts to replace the original event. In
order to believe in the novelty of the new day the poet must once
again differentiate between virtually identical phenomena
("nada es igual ni se repite"). Once again he does so tentatively,
affirming and at the same time calling into question his own
affirmation. His need to emphasize the originality of one particular dawn stems from his awareness of the many identical past
and future revelations of the light:

Todo es nuevo quizá. Si no lo fuera,
si en medio de esta hora las imágenes
cobraran vida en otras, y con ellas
los recuerdos de un día ya pasado
volvieran ocultando el de hoy, volvieran
aclarándolo, sí, pero ocultando
su claridad naciente, ¿qué sorpresa

le daría a mi ser, qué devaneo,
qué nueva luz o qué labores nuevas?

· · · · · · · · · · · ·
                           Qué verdad, qué limpia escena
la del amor, que nunca ve en las cosas
la triste realidad de su apariencia.

Everything is new perhaps. If it weren't,
if in the middle of this hour the images
took on a life in other lives, and with them
the memories of an already past day
returned, hiding that of today, returned ·
lighting it up, yes, but hiding
its clarity being born, what a surprise
it would give to my being, what dizziness,
what new light or what new labors?

· · · · · · · · · · · · ·
                           What truth, what clean scene
that of love, that never sees in things
the sad reality of their appearance.

Previous repetitions of the event threaten to cast a shadow over
the novelty of the new day. The brightness of other dawns
obscures the particularity of *this* dawn. Cycles of images from the
past can be superimposed upon the present, so that the poet
loses his capacity to distinguish the new from the old. The result,
as might be expected, is a new confusion indistinguishable from
that of past crises. The poet's attempt to renew and thus preserve
his vision leads him into another repetition of the same cycle
that has disillusioned him many times before.

    The final exclamation, "todo es nuevo quizá," reaffirms the
poetics of vision but also reveals the deep division in the poet's
thought. Truth and reality, usually almost synonymous, become
antithetical. The interpretive crisis is the result, ultimately, or the
alternation of two irreconcilable points of view: an ability to see
beyond surface appearances ("la triste realidad") in order to
reach the truth, and the pressure to renounce this vision so as to
participate in the world in a more authentic way. Since dawn
threatens the poet's capacity to discover the truth, he must
choose whether to preserve his knowledge of the duplicity of
language or to renounce this knowledge and his own distance
from nature, from what, for the visionary poet, is merely "la triste
realidad de su apariencia."

    The third poem of the first section is an explicit commentary
on this dilemma. A tree represents the spontaneity and thus the
unconsciousness of nature:

La encina, que conserva más un rayo
de sol que todo un mes de primavera,
no siente lo espontáneo de su sombra,
la sencillez del crecimiento; apenas
si conoce el terreno en que ha brotado.

(1º III, 35)

The oak, which conserves more of a sunbeam
than an entire spring month,
does not feel the spontaneity of its shadow,
the simplicity of growth; it hardly
knows the terrain in which it has sprung.

The poet anthropomorphizes the oak tree in order to interpret it as an alter ego. He would like to attain the tree's natural innocence, while the tree, in its turn, seeks to transcend its own limitations, to become a poet. In a movement of reciprocal identification the human being and the tree exchange their characteristics. The poet imagines what it would be like to be a tree imagining what it would be like to be a poet. The tree and poet represent two moments of the same cycle. The poet moves downward to identify himself with the unreflective life of the oak. As the tree identifies with its surroundings, however, it begins an upward movement, away from itself and toward the heavens. Like the poet, it seeks to distinguish between the multiple phenomenon of the world. This cycle, it turns out, is another version of the cycle of night and day, or of the circular movement of the dawn itself. The sowing of the seed, a part of the natural cycle of death and rebirth, is also the emergence of the poet's vision. These two metaphors for the dawn are potentially contradictory, however, for the first involves a sacrifice of the poet's human thought, while the second implies its triumph. The last lines of the poem consist of a series of contradictory rhetorical questions:

Y es cierto, pues la encina ¿qué sabría
de la muerte sin mí? ¿Y acaso es cierta
su intimidad, su instinto, lo espóntaneo
de su sombra más fiel que nadie? ¿Es cierta
mi vida así, en sus persistentes hojas,
a medio descrifrar la primavera?

And it is certain, for the oak, what would it know
of death without me? And are they perhaps certain,
its intimacy, its instinct, the spontaneity
of its shadow, more faithful than anyone? Is my life

certain like this, in its persistent leaves,
the spring half deciphered?

This conclusion vacillates between two perspectives: the human knowledge of the poet and the innocent (unknowing) spontaneity of the tree. Neither point of view can be privileged, for each implies a critique of the other: just as the oak cannot be aware of its own death, so the human being's knowledge cuts him off from spontaneous participation in nature. The poem ends in the air: the poet's life cannot be safe, sure, or certain because he has not yet interpreted the spring, resolved this play of contradictory perspectives. The reader of the poem cannot reach a fixed interpretation when the poet himself is still engaged in the process of reading the world.

Although the majority of the poems in *Don de la ebriedad* reflect the tension between vision and the sacrifice of vision, between crisis and resolution, the sequence as a whole shows a way to escape from this uncertainty. There *is* a possible exit from the cycle of self-consuming images: the poet can choose instead to sacrifice his own ego and join the more genuine cycle of mortal life and death. A few key poems tip the balance in favor of this alternative. In contrast to the irresolution of the poems of crisis, these poems employ a rhetoric of certainty that has led many readers to conclude that the book as a whole is the naive expression of its author's youthful exuberance and direct experience of the natural world.

A crucial feature of what I have called visionary poetics is the alienation of the poetic subject. The poet is able to see beyond the deceptive darkness precisely because he is *not* integrated into the world. The final stage in the story of the dawn is a movement toward a sacrifice of the ego: the poet expresses the desire to relinquish his own self so that he may become the integrated part of a larger whole. This stage comes last—not in the order in which the poems appear in the book, but rather in the order of the paradoxical narrative logic of the sequence as a whole. As the resolution of the crisis, it provides the poem with an end point; it marks the complete reversal of the original visionary poetics. Before the dawn, language was the ideal medium for the revelation of the truth behind deceptive appearances. The final sacrifice of the self implies a sacrifice, as well, of human language. In order to achieve integration into the natural order, the poet's voice must become identical with nature's own signs.

The quest for an end to language through language itself is

always paradoxical. Taken at his word, the poet should simply stop writing, no longer make the effort to transcend his temporal condition through the poetic word. For Rodríguez, nevertheless, language is the only means to participate in the world, even though it inevitably stands in the way of this participation. It is because he cannot take for granted a direct, unmediated relationship to nature, as many of his commentators have done, that the poet needs language even as he appears to reject it. Nature in *Don de la ebriedad* is always linguistic, whether it is the veil of deceptive appearances, the darkness that conceals the night, or the true language of the day. The poet aspires to transform his own speech into this more genuine system of signs:

> Cuándo hablaré de ti sin voz de hombre
> para no acabar nunca, como el río
> no acaba de contar su pena y tiene
> dichas ya más palabras que yo mismo.
>
> (1º V, 36)

> When will I speak of you without a man's voice
> so as never to finish, as the river
> never finishes telling its sorrow and has said
> more words already than myself.

The speaker of this poem does not claim to have achieved such a natural language but rather anticipates it in an indefinite future. It is clear as well that he has not escaped from the visionary crisis, the cycle of images of his poetic drunkenness. The context of this plea for an end to his human voice is provided precisely by the uncertainty of the interpretive crisis. The clearest connection between this crisis and the ultimate rejection of language is in the final lines of this same poem:

> Cuándo hablaré de ti sin voz de hombre.
> Cuándo. Mi boca sólo llega al signo,
> sólo interpreta muy confusamente.
> Y es que hay duras verdades de un continuo
> crecer, hay esperanzas que no logran
> sobrepasar el tiempo y convertirlo
> en seca fuente de llanura, como
> hay terrenos que no filtran el limo.
>
> (1º V, 37)

> When will I speak of you without a man's voice.
> When. My mouth only arrives at the sign,

only interprets very confusedly.
And it is that there are hard truths of continuous
flow, there are hopes that do not succeed
in overtaking time and converting it
into a dry source on the plain, as
there are terrains that do not filter the mud.

It is because the poet has a "man's voice" that he remains within the cycle. This voice is prone to doubt because of its uncertain position between transcendent vision and immanent nature. To resolve the crisis caused by his intermediate state, the poet must seek either to become a part of nature and time or to escape his temporal destiny. In the poem beginning "Cuándo hablaré de ti sin voz de hombre" the solution to the crisis of vision is still ambiguous: the alternative to a human voice could be either the natural voice of the river or, on the contrary, the superhuman language of the moment before creation. But this attempt to preserve a visionary poetics is a failure almost by definition, for the poet's transcendent vision is inherently duplicitous: it contains the seeds of its own crisis. The "success" of vision in the final poem of *Don de la ebriedad* paradoxically brings an explicit repudiation of the timeless state of alienation from nature. One could say that the poet is too successful in his effort to "sobrepasar el tiempo y convertirlo / en seca fuente de llanura":

> Cómo veo los árboles ahora.
> No con hojas caedizas, no con ramas
> sujetas a la voz del crecimiento.
> Y hasta a la brisa que los quema a ráfagas
> no la siento como algo de la tierra
> ni del cielo tampoco, sino falta
> de ese dolor de vida con destino.
>
> (3º VIII, 63)

> How do I see the trees now.
> Not with leaves likely to fall, not with branches
> subject to the voice of growth.
> And even the breeze that burns them in gusts
> I don't feel it as something of the earth
> or of the sky either, but as a lack
> of that pain of a life with destiny.

The poet's vision converts the world into an eternally frozen landscape where neither death nor life, equally crucial in the temporal cycle of nature, have a place. As in the first poem of the book, "Siempre la claridad viene del cielo," this vision stands above the objects seen:

> Y a los campos, al mar, a las montañas
> muy por encima de su clara forma
> los veo. ¿Qué me han hecho en la mirada?
> ¿Es que voy a morir? Decidme ¿cómo
> veis a los hombres, a sus obras, almas
> inmortales? Sí, ebrio estoy, sin duda.
> La mañana no es tal, es una amplia
> llanura sin combate, casi eterna,
> casi desconocida porque en cada
> lugar donde antes era sombra el tiempo,
> ahora la luz espera ser creada.

> And the fields, the sea, the mountains
> much above their clear form
> I see them. What have they done to my gaze?
> Is it that I will die? Tell me, how
> do you see men, their works, immortal
> souls? Yes, I am drunk, without a doubt.
> The morning is not a morning, it is a wide
> plain without combat, almost eternal,
> almost unknown because in each
> place where before time was a shadow,
> now the light waits to be created.

Unlike the paradoxical dawn of other poems, at once an unchanging state and a temporal event, this eternal vision is no longer bound to time. The poet sees the morning with the vision of an "immortal soul," as a single, undivided unity. Whereas night and day usually overlap, so that the poet can never coincide with the revelation itself, in this poem he envisions a moment *between*: it is no longer night ("antes era sombra el tiempo") and it is not yet day ("ahora la luz espera ser creada"). The wind, a disembodied and unstable force analogous to the light, moves ever more rapidly in a circular movement in order to reach a still point, to coincide with its own breath:

> No sólo el aire deja más su aliento:
> no posee ni cántico ni nada;
>
> . . . .
> Pues bien: el aire de hoy tiene su cántico.
> ¡Si lo oye seis! Y el sol, et fuego, el agua,

cómo dan posesión a estos mis ojos.
¿Es que voy a vivir? ¿Tan pronto acaba
la ebriedad? Ay, y como veo ahora
los árboles, qué pocos días faltan . . .

Not only the air leaves behind its breath any longer:
it doesn't possess a canticle or anything else;
. . . .
Well, the air of today has its canticle.
If you could hear it! And the sun, the fire, the water,
how they give possession to these, my eyes.
Is it that I am going to live? Does drunkenness
end so soon? Ah, and how I see
the trees now, how few days remain . . .

The poet is able to possess the world, for it is motionless and at one with itself. Paradoxically, it is at this moment, the fulfillment of his vision, that the poet is able to forsee an end to the visionary cycle of poetic drunkenness. His realization of his own mortality ("¿Es que voy a morir?") also makes him aware of his life as a human being. His very success as a visionary poet—a vision of a dead landscape—obliges him to renounce his attempts to remain apart from nature.

Like the poem beginning "Cómo veo los árboles," the lyric that closes the first book of Don points toward an end to the visionary cycle. In this poem the poet takes a different strategy: instead of showing the impasse of vision, he seeks to forget that it ever existed, making his least ambivalent call for a "natural" voice:

Como si nunca hubiera sido mía
dad al aire mi voz y que en el aire
sea de todos y la sepan todos
igual que una mañana o una tarde.

(1º IX, 40)

As if they had never been mine
give to the air my voice and in the air
let it be for all and let all know it
just like a morning or an afternoon.

The sacrifice of the self is an unrealized desire which is only possible in terms of a fictional premise: that the poet's ego has never been separated from nature, that his language has never alienated him from the world. Like the eternal vision that is the poet's initial ideal, this state of selflessness exists only in a hypothetical future. The poet seeks to become another part of creation rather than a privileged creator:

> Ni a la rama tan sólo abril acude
> ni el agua espera sólo el estiaje.
> ¿Quién podría decir que es suyo el viento,
> suya la luz, el canto de las aves
> en que esplende la estación, más cuando
> llega la noche y en los chopos arde
> tan peligrosamente retenida?

> April does not come only to the branch
> nor does the low waterpoint await only the water.
> Who could say that the wind is his,
> his the light, the song of the birds
> in which the season blooms, even more when
> night arrives and in the poplars burns
> so dangerously retained?

The central image of *Don*, the night as a potential day, represents in these lines the imminent sacrifice of the self rather than an egoistic vision:

> ¡Que todo acabe aquí, que todo acabe
> de una vez para siempre! La flor vive
> tan bella porque vive poco tiempo
> y, sin embargo, cómo se da, unánime,
> dejando de ser flor y convirtiéndose
> en ímpetu de entrega.

> Let it all end here, let everything end
> once and forever! The flower lives
> so beautifully because it lives so little time
> and, nevertheless, how it gives itself, unanimously,
> being no longer a flower and converting itself
> into impetus of surrender.

Like the light of day, identified with the poet's vision, language, and desire, the flower's beauty stems from its precariousness. Rather than immortalizing its fleeting beauty or lamenting its destruction, the poet celebrates its *entrega*, or surrender. Its fulfillment is not to become a self-contained monument to itself but rather to give itself up. In the final lines of the poem the poet identifies himself directly with the flower and calls on the winter to be his executioner:

> Invierno, aunque
> no esté detrás la primavera, saca
> fuera de mí lo mío y hazme parte,
> inútil polen que se cae en tierra
> pero ha sido de todos y de nadie.
>
> . . . .
>
> qué sacrilegio este del cuerpo, este
> de no poder ser hostia para darse.

> Winter, although
> spring might not follow, take
> out of me what is mine and make me a part,
> useless pollen that falls on the earth
> but has belonged to all and to none.
>
> . . . .
>
> What a sacrilege to have a body,
> unable to be a host to give oneself up.

The impulse toward the dissolution of the body in the final
lines—the poet complains that his flesh cannot be a eucharist to
be given up in sacrifice—is an exact inversion of the celebration
of the dawn as the incarnation of the poet's desire:

> Limpio deseo cada vez más mío
> cada vez menos vuestro, hasta que llegue
> por fin a ser mi sangre y mi tarea
> corpóreo como el sol cuando amanece.
>
> (1ªIV, 36)

> A clean desire more and more mine
> less and less yours, until it succeeds
> at last in being my blood and my task
> corporeal as the sun when it dawns.

The transformation of visionary poetics into its opposite is complete. Egoism has become selflessness, pride humility. In the
Christian subtext of *Don de la ebriedad*, the incarnation has
given way to the crucifixion, and the poet awaits his rebirth. The
desire to preserve an eternal version of the self through language
has given way to a surrender to time and a renunciation of a
privileged poetic speech.

A careful analysis of the rhetoric of sacrifice demonstrates that
the poet has not yet escaped from the double bind of language.
Such a resolution of the crisis can take place only outside of the

poem, in a natural state toward which he can only gesture from within his linguistic prison. The appeal to simplicity is deceptive, for the poem depends for its rhetorical forcefulness upon the very same linguistic resources against which it protests. It stakes its claims in a language that signals its own distance from the world. In the first sentence alone there is a negative, contrary-to-fact condition, followed by a command, a wish expressed in the subjunctive, and a simile.

If the poet has not escaped from language, then neither has the reader. The poem appeals to the reader, implicitly, to sacrifice his or her own self, but at the same time it demonstrates the difficulty of doing so. In a passage that applies strikingly well to *Don de la ebriedad*, Stanley Fish has characterized the poetry of George Herbert in terms of a tension between the need to preserve the ego and the pressure to give it up:

> There is nothing easy about the "letting go" this poetry requires of us. We are, after all, being asked to acquiesce in the discarding of those very habits of thought and mind that preserve our dignity by implying our independence. Naturally (the word is double-edged) we resist, and our resistance is often mirrored in the obstinate questionings and remonstrations of the first-person voice. The result is a poetics of tension, reflecting a continuing dialectic between an ego-centric vision which believes in, and is sustained by, the distinctions it creates, and the relentless pressure of a resolving and dissolving insight.[12]

The question that remains is that of the reader's response to this tension: does he or she resist "the relentless pressure of a resolving and dissolving insight" or surrender to it and, at least temporarily, "let go" of the self?[13]

"Como si nunca hubiera sido mía," a favorite of critics and readers alike, appeals strongly to the idea of a more direct connection to nature, even though a close analysis of its rhetoric would reveal that the poet is still an alienated being. Many readers, taking this poem as representative, have understood the sacrifice of the self to be the final meaning of *Don de la ebriedad*. Instead of an unfulfilled desire for communion with the natural world, expressed in the same poetic language that obstructs any such communion, these readers hear the voice of the countryside itself. Here is José Luis Cano, one of the first critics to comment on the work:

> Una juventud recién estrenada, que había crecido en el abierto campo zamorano, escuchando el raudo sonar del Duero, bebiendo aire alto y puro, rompía a cantar con una voz segura, muy densa de savias y aromas. *Don de la ebriedad* era un solo y largo poema, estremecido de amor a la luz, al aire, al campo libre y virgen.[14]

> A youthfulness that had just had its debut, that had grown in the open Zamoran countryside listening to the rapid sound of the river Duero, drinking high, pure air, was breaking into song with a sure voice, very dense with saps and odors. *Don de la ebriedad* was a single long poem, trembling with love for the light, the air, the free and virgin countryside.

This exalted tone reveals a lack of distance from the rhetoric of the poems themselves. Claudio Rodríguez himself offers a similar reading. Although he protests at the beginning of his prologue to *Desde mis poemas* that his distance from his own earlier work prevents him from explicating it adequately, his problem is actually the reverse. It is not that he cannot relive his former state of consciousness but rather that he cannot escape from it. His commentary on his first book of poems, like that of Cano, echoes the rhetorical innocence of the poems themselves.

> Dos datos suficientes para orientar al lector. Poesía—adolescencia—como un don; y ebriedad como un estado de entusiasmo. . . . Claro está que no puedo reproducir dichas sensaciones, pero sí aclarar que mis primeros poemas brotaron del contacto directo, vivido, recorrido, con la realidad de mi tierra, con la geografía y con el pulso de la gente castellana, zamorana.[15]

> Two facts are sufficient to orient the reader. Poetry—adolescence— as a gift; and drunkenness as a state of enthusiasm. . . . It is clear that I cannot reproduce these sensations, but I can make it clear that my first poems sprung up from a direct, lived, traveled contact with the reality of my land, with the geography and the pulse of the Castilian, the Zamoran people.

José Luis Cano's pastoral reading of *Don de la ebriedad*, seconded by the author himself, typifies the prevalent critical opinion of the work. Rather than immediately discounting this view for its naiveté, scoring an easy rhetorical point against a vulnerable position, it would be useful to account for the process by which the text has led so many of its readers to a similar conclusion. There is an inherent conflict, as Jonathan Culler has argued in "Beyond interpretation," between the attempt to explain how the reader makes sense of a text and the desire to outdo previous readers and produce better interpretations. Other critics' readings are not so much incorrect interpretations as they are a part of the phenomenon to be explained.[16]

The reader's experience of the more difficult poems of crisis is one of disorientation and confusion. He or she is caught up in the same visionary crisis as the poet within the text. An interpretation that took into account the experience I am positing would avoid the reduction of this complex play of perspectives to a simple communion with the world. At the same time, the poet's interpretive crisis is not necessarily an end in itself. Adopting Stanley Fish's words, I have characterized these poems as "self-consuming artifacts." Although Fish privileges the temporal experience of reading over the closure of interpretation, the final extraction of meaning, his term could also imply that the reader's experience is itself subverted. The method of analysis proposed in "Literature in the Reader: Affective Stylistics," the last chapter of his book, distorts Fish's own practice as a reader:

> In the analysis of a reading experience, when does one come to the point? The answer is "never," or, no sooner than the pressure to do so becomes unbearable (psychologically). Coming to the point is the goal of criticism that believes in content, in extractable meaning, in the utterance as a repository. Coming to a point fulfills a need that most literature deliberately frustrates (if we open ourselves to it), the need to simplify and close.[17]

The experience of attempting to make sense of the text involves the constant frustration of the reader's need to interpret. Yet in practice the deferral of meaning is usually provisional: Fish's favored texts call themselves into question in the name of another reality outside of language. The self-consuming artifact, in other words, aims to move the reader beyond the very process that the critic wishes to preserve. The poetry of George Herbert, for example, forces the reader to abandon his or her independence of mind, to "let go" of self. Fish, in effect, asks the reader to resist the principal thrust of such a work *away from itself.* He values for its own sake an experience that the text shows to be ultimately inadequate.[18]

The reader of *Don de la ebriedad* faces the dilemma of having to deny either the experience of reading or else the "final meaning" of the work. The poem *consumes itself,* arriving at a conclusion that appears to detach itself from the problematics of poetic vision. The traditional opposition between temporal reading and timeless interpretation, which also forms the basis of Fish's theory, breaks down: the reader's struggle to make sense of the text mirrors the poet's efforts to preserve an eternal self, whereas the conclusion, the end-product of reading, is a surrender to time. The two major approaches to *Don*, then, can be explained as versions of interpretive strategies that take place within the text. Some readers adopt the tone of "Como si nunca hubiera sido mía / dad al aire mi voz," while others identify with the poet's more skeptical voice: "Mi boca sólo llega al signo, / sólo interpreta muy confusamente." Critics such as José Luis Cano, who assert the innocence and naturalness of the poet, almost invariably employ an exalted, quasi-poetic style that echoes the poet's own desire to attain such a state. Any real analysis would be fatal to their assumption: they can only take for granted that the text is naive by maintaining their own blindness. A reader who does not accept the self-destruction of the crisis of dawn will, in effect, remain within the eternal cycle of vision and re-vision from which the poet desires to escape. Martha LaFollette Miller, for example, depicts the process of reading "Siempre la claridad viene del cielo" as a search for meaning that ultimately leads to an impasse, when the reader becomes aware of the failure of language to represent reality.[19]

The dialectic of these two opposing strategies for interpreting the text reflects the dialectic of two conceptions of language. The attempt to preserve the "eternal" view of the dawn as a state of tension between darkness and light, deception and truth, leads to an endless cycle of revelation and crisis. The language of nature, in which there is no division between signifier and signified, corresponds to the more authentic, temporal cycle of death and rebirth. What is at stake is not the relation of words to a nonverbal reality but rather the interrelation between two systems of signs, each of which calls the other into question. The poet's language unveils the light hidden within the shadows, piercing through the deceptive appearances of things, whereas the transparent signs of nature expose the inauthenticity of this human speech.

The two strategies of reading, and the ideas of the sign they imply, cannot easily be reconciled. Their divergence extends to their fundamentally different conceptions of the *form* of the work. The privileging of the eternal cycle makes *Don* an endlessly repeating cycle of poems, which the reader can stop reading but never *finish*. If the reader accepts the poet's conversion to the temporal cycle, on the other hand, then the work becomes a narrative sequence with a beginning, middle, and end: he or she can complete it and put it aside.[20] In my view *Don* is neither an endless cycle nor a narrative sequence but a transition from one type of form to the other, the story of the poet's conversion to a new theory of the sign. Dawn is a paradoxical event because it marks a point of intersection not only of two visions of language but also of two opposing ways of ordering thought: the logical and the narrative.[21] Before the dawn the day is *implicit* within the light. It follows as one idea "follows" from another. As an event in time, however, the day simply comes after the night. The sequence as a whole is an effort to come to terms in one way or another with this simple but radical redefinition.

My own reading of *Don de la ebriedad* has not escaped the dilemma I have described. My basic assumption has been that the poems demand to be understood as a coherent work rather than as a collection of anthology pieces: virtually every poem presents a different version of the same central event. Yet Claudio Rodríguez's first book resists a unified reading even as it invites one. As a parable of the process of interpretation, it dramatizes a transition between two diametrically opposed theories of the sign. The poet—a reader within the poem—moves from a transcendent, eternalizing vision toward an unmediated participation in time and nature. The reader of the text must choose whether to accept the poet's final plunge into the world or to continue to struggle with the crisis of visionary poetics.

3

The Motive for Metaphor: *Conjuros* and the Rhetoric of Social Solidarity

> Put identification and division ambiguously together, so that you cannot know for certain just where one ends and the other begins, and you have the characteristic invitation to rhetoric.
>
> —Kenneth Burke

It is in *Conjuros* (Incantations), published in 1958, that Rodríguez first comes to terms with one of the central problems of postwar Spanish poetry: the poet's social responsibility. In contrast to *Don de la ebriedad,* a brilliant but historically anomalous work, this second volume of poems can be read as a response to the "poesía social" that dominated literary life during the period. The best introduction to this movement defines "social poetry" in terms of its political ideology: "only those who believed in social change through political means, and used their poetic activity to lend a helping hand in the battle for a better society, are to be considered as fully social poets."[1] This assertion is historically accurate: in the coded terminology of postwar literature the word *social* was used as a euphemism for *political.* To limit the social to the political in this way, however, is to exclude the less explicitly ideological poets of the period, such as Rodríguez and Vicente Aleixandre, who share a central aim of the "social poets": not necessarily to change the world but to establish a bond of communication with their audience.

Much of the "social poetry" written in Spain in the postwar period, in effect, is primarily concerned with an essentially rhetorical problem: the poet's identification with an ideal audience. The actual protest against oppressive political conditions, the ostensible aim of such poetry, plays a surprisingly secondary part in comparison to the poet's self-conscious reflection on his or her own role as a social poet, speaking to and on behalf of the "immense majority," to quote a phrase made famous by Blas de Otero. "It would not be totally inexact to say that he writes mostly *about* social poetry," Daydí-Tolson has observed of Otero, "rather than writing social poetry itself."[2]

Rodríguez's attitude toward social poetry, like that of the majority of the poets of his generation, is highly ambivalent. In this respect, Rodríguez's response is typical of a group of younger writers who sympathize, in broad terms, with the social aims of the older generation while seeing their aesthetic premises as extremely inadequate. Writing in 1963, Rodríguez acknowledges the importance of his older, more committed colleagues in making all poets more aware of their political responsibilities. He recognizes, however, that their approach to the problem is insufficient in both aesthetic and social terms. Rodríguez's *social* critique of the social poets is potentially more damning than his purely aesthetic critique, since these poets aspire to sociopolitical action. He calls into question the political efficacy of poets who claim to put politics first. The "dramatic paradox" of social poetry, according to Rodríguez, is that the common man does not or cannot read the poetry written in his name: "Se siente el vértigo, la ineficacia y la vergüenza del que habla sin auditorio o imaginándose un auditorio fantasma" [One feels the vertigo, the ineffectiveness and the shame of one who speaks without an audience or imagining a phantom audience].[3]

The poet of *Conjuros*, like the poetic voice in the work of the "social poets," desires to identify himself with his community, to overcome the differences that keep him apart from those whom he addresses. Returning to his native city, from which he has been estranged, his aim is to become a part of an ideal social order that remains in harmony with nature. He attempts to persuade both the real reader of the text and his projected audience, the people of his city, of his worthiness to rejoin this community. At the same time he is more conscious of the fictionality of this social solidarity. Many critics of *Conjuros* have assumed that Rodríguez is naively and enthusiastically celebrating the ordinary life of the countryside around Zamora.[4] By taking for granted what in fact is most in question, the poet's natural place within a social order based on nature, they are uncritically echoing the rhetoric of the text. The poet's identification with his community is not a reflection of a reality that exists prior to language; it is, rather, a symbolic act that takes place within *Conjuros* itself.[5] In the course of the work the poet himself comes to a realization of the rhetorical nature of his project. A "social

poet," in the more restricted sense of the term, could not openly
acknowledge that his or her identification with an ideal audience
is a fiction, for to do so would be to renounce any claim to
efficacy in the sociopolitical realm. Rodríguez, in contrast,
openly calls this myth into question. Throughout *Conjuros* the
poet develops a system of interconnected analogies that serve to
identify his community with the natural world. The same figurative language, however, that promises to unite human beings
and nature also reveals the differences between them. The rhetorical medium through which the poet had hoped to establish
his bond with a natural society ultimately exposes the il-
lusoriness of this project. His audience is a phantom; the social
solidarity of his community is based not on nature but on mutual
distrust and fear.

Rodríguez's demystification of social poetry must also be understood in terms of the development of his own work. Several
key poems of *Don de la ebriedad,* analyzed in the previous
chapter, propose the ideal of an uncritical participation in the
world of nature as an antidote to the alienation implicit in the
timeless, transcendent vision. This participation implies a certain linguistic innocence, that is, a deliberate forgetting of the
arbitrary nature of the sign. At the same time, this participation
takes place by means of language, since the poet does not literally stop writing. In Kenneth Burke's terms, it can be defined as a
"symbolic action," as a rhetorical attempt to alter reality by
manipulating language itself. It is this contradiction—between
the seemingly antilinguistic ideal of participation and the symbolic nature of the act—that comes to a head in *Conjuros.* If *Don
de la ebriedad* involves a crisis of visionary poetics, Rodríguez's
second book leads to a crisis of the opposite ideal: the rhetoric of
participation.
    The first step in the symbolic action of *Conjuros* is a redefini-
tion of the ideal of poetic participation first developed in
Rodríguez's previous book. The poet of *Don de la ebriedad* desires to become an integrated part of the natural world, to lose his
human consciousness so as to become identical with a river or a
tree. This involves a specifically linguistic transformation, a rhetorical appeal to the identification of language with reality. In the
poems that open *Conjuros* the poet rewrites this cluster of
motives in explicitly social terms. His goal now is to integrate
himself into a community that itself is based directly on nature,

to sacrifice his individual ego in the name of a "natural" social solidarity.

Since the poet does not abandon the idea that nature is the ultimate source of authenticity, he expresses his desire for social solidarity in the natural imagery characteristic of *Don*. The first poem in *Conjuros*, "A la respiración en la llanura" [To breathing on the plain], asks its audience to surrender itself in the natural world:

> ¡Dejad de respirar y que os respire
> la tierra, que os enciende en sus pulmones
> maravillosos! Mire
> quien mire, ¿no verá en las estaciones
> un rastro como de aire que se alienta?[6]

> Stop breathing and let the earth
> breathe you, let it light you on fire in its marvellous
> lungs! Look
> whoever might, will he not see in the seasons
> a trace as if of air that feeds itself?

In the poems of *Don* the poet is essentially alone in the landscape. His implicit reader is another poet or like-minded soul similarly solitary in his or her relation to the natural world. In this poem, however, the speaker addresses his audience in the plural form rather than the singular that is so frequently used in the earlier book. As in *Don*, the poet expresses the desire to sacrifice his ego in order to become an integrated part of a greater, more inclusive world. His symbolic death will bring about his purification and reintegration into nature:

> Sería natural aquí la muerte.
> No se tendría en cuenta,
> como la luz, como el espacio, ¡Muerte
> con sólo respirar! Fuera de día
> ahora y me quedaría sin sentido
> en estos campos, y respiraría
> hondo como estos árboles, sin ruido.
> Por eso la mañana aún es un vuelo
> creciente y alto sobre
> los montes, y un impulso a ras del suelo
> que antes de que se efunda y de que cobre
> forma ya es surco para el nuevo grano.

(69)

> Death would be natural here.
> It would not be noticed,
> like light, like space, Death
> with breathing alone! Were it day
> now and I would remain senseless
> in these fields, and I would breathe
> deep like these trees, without sound.
> Because of this the morning is still a flight
> growing and high above
> the hilltops, and an impulse parallel to the ground
> that before it effuses and takes on
> form is already a furrow for the new grain.

These lines would not be out of place in *Don*. The rhetorical appeal to loss of consciousness, and the double image of the sunrise as a flight and as a furrow in the earth, are frequent in the earlier book. As this poem progresses, however, the natural scene becomes a metaphor for a human community. The world in which the poet loses his ego now includes his listeners, who are at once participants in the poet's natural communion and a part of nature itself:

> Oh, mi aposento. Qué riego del alma
> éste con el que doy mi vida y gano
> tantas vidas hermosas. Tened calma
> los que me respiráis, hombres y cosas.
> Soy vuestro. Sois también vosotros míos.
>
> Oh, my dwelling place. What watering of the soul
> is this with which I give my life and gain
> so many beautiful lives. Be calm
> you who breathe me, men and things.
> I am yours. You are also mine.

The speaker directs his voice simultaneously to man and to nature, "hombres y cosas." Apostrophe is one of the characteristic figures of speech in *Conjuros*: the titles of many poems address themselves to inanimate objects rather than to the human audience: "Al ruido del Duero" (To the sound of the Duero), "A mi ropa tendida" (To my hanging clothes), "A la nube aquella" (To that cloud). The effect of this trope is to identify the social order and the natural world; by calling on human beings and things in the same breath, the poet abolishes the distance between them.

The lines that follow could easily be from *Don de la ebriedad*:

Cómo aumentan las rosas
su juventud al entregarse. ¡Abríos
a todo! El heno estalla en primavera,
el pino da salud con su olor fuerte.
¡Qué hostia la del aliento, qué manera
de crear, qué taller claro de muerte!

                                                    (69–70)

How the roses enlarge
their youth as they surrender themselves. Open up
to everything! Hay bursts in springtime,
the pine gives health with its strong odor.
What a host is this breath, what manner
of creation, what clear workshop of death.

The images of the rose and the communion wafer recall the last
poem of the first section of Rodríguez's earlier book:

        qué sacrilegio éste del cuerpo, éste
        de no poder ser hostia para darse.   (1º IX, 40)

        what a sacrilege to have a body,
        unable to be a host in order to give oneself up.

The difference is in the context. The poet of *Conjuros* reinterprets
this natural imagery in social terms; his communion with nature
has become a union with his fellow human beings as well.

   Rodríguez's vision of social solidarity owes a great deal to
Vicente Aleixandre, to whom *Conjuros* is dedicated. Although
Rodríguez's work rarely echoes that of other poets directly, the
concluding lines of "A la respiración en la llanura" are a significant exception:

        No sé cómo he vivido
        hasta ahora ni en qué cuerpo he sentido
        pero algo me levanta al día puro,
        me comunica un corazón inmenso,
        como el de la meseta, y mi conjuro
        es el del aire, tenso
        por la respiración del campo henchida
        muy cerca de mi alma en el momento
        en que pongo la vida
        al voraz paso de cualquier aliento.

                                                    (70)

I do not know how I have lived
until now nor in what body I have felt
but something raises me to the pure day,
communicates to me an immense heart
like that of the plain, and my incantation
is that of the air, tense
with the breathing of the swollen countryside
very close to my soul in the moment
in which I put my life
to the voracious step of any breath.

The "corazón inmenso" here evokes the concluding lines of a
poem from Aleixandre's *Historia del corazón* (1954): "¡Oh pe-
queño corazón diminuto, corazón que quiere latir / para ser él
también el unánime corazón que le alcanza!" [Oh small, dimin-
utive heart, heart that wants to beat / to be he too the unanimous
heart that reaches him.][7] Rodríguez's speaker, like the protagonist
of Aleixandre's poem, renounces his egoism in favor of a selfless
participation in the world. The use of the word "comunica"
suggests a reinterpretation of the ideal of *comunicación* that is
central to the poetics of Aleixandre as well as of the "social
poets." On one level this term can refer to the transmission of
content through a transparent medium, in opposition to the more
complex workings of language. Rodríguez, along with other poets
of his generation, rejects the notion that poetry is "merely" communication in this narrow sense. A second way of understanding
the term, though, is to relate it to words such as "común,"
"comunión," and "comunidad." The definitions of the Latin verb
communicare, the root of both the English and the Spanish
words, reveal that communication can be a synonym for participation and even union: "to make common; to communicate,
impart, share; to share in, take part in; to unite, connect, join."
These meanings are all relevant to the project of social identification in *Conjuros*. The poet communicates with his fellow human
beings not by transmitting information to them but by establishing a common bond with them, by becoming a part of their
community. I believe that Rodríguez actually goes beyond Aleixandre, not to mention the social poets, in establishing a mysticism of solidarity with strong Christian connotations. He thus
takes the social to a new dimension, only implicit in the work of
the older poets. This is evident in his use of Christian imagery,
especially the communion wafer *(hostia)* as a symbol for the
sacrifice of the ego and the subsequent consolidation of the

community. It should not be forgotten that the etymology of the term *religion* is "binding together."

Other poems in the first section of the book further develop the link between social and natural solidarity suggested by the conclusion of "A la respiración en la llanura." "A las estrellas" (To the stars), the second poem in the book, resembles "A la respiración" in that it gives a social interpretation to the natural imagery and the sacrifice of the ego so characteristic of Rodríguez's earlier poetry. Several other poems relate social solidarity to the practice of agriculture. Whereas nature in *Don de la ebriedad* tends to appear as a force beyond human control, in *Conjuros* the dominant system of metaphors stresses the cooperation of society and nature through the cultivation of the earth.[8]

"A las puertas de la ciudad" ("At the city gates," or "To the city gates"), standing at the center of the first "book" of *Conjuros*, makes explicit the metaphorical link between the human community and the natural world. The beginning of the poem presents the poet in an ambivalent position, hesitating outside the city yet drawn inexorably toward it:

> Voy a esperar un poco
> hasta que se ponga el sol, aunque estos pasos
> se me vayan allí, hacia el baile mío,
> hacia la vida mía.

(74)

> I am going to wait a while
> until the sun goes down, although these steps
> take me there, toward my dance,
> toward my life.

The poet's desire to purify himself through self-sacrifice, seen already in "A la respiración" and "A las estrellas," implies the existence of guilt. The source of this guilt lies in the poet's rejection of his community:

> Tantos años
> hice buena pareja con vosotros,
> amigos. Y os dejé, y me fui a mi barrio
> de juventud creyendo
> que allí estaría mi verbena en vano.
> ¡Si creí que podíais seguir siempre

> con la seca impiedad, con el engaño
> de la ciudad a cuestas! ¡Si creía
> que ella, la bien cercada, mal cercado
> os tuvo siempre el corazón . . .
>
>   So many years
> I was a good partner to all of you,
> friends. And I left you, and I went to my
> youthful neighborhood believing
> that there my festival would be in vain.
> Why, I believed that you could continue always
> with the dry irreverence, with the deceit
> of the city on your backs! Why, I believed
> that she, the well-enclosed, had always badly
> enclosed your heart . . .

More specifically, his original sin is his very consciousness of the duplicity of language, a consciousness which made him unable to read the transparent signs of his native city:

>   . . . y era
> todo sencillo, todo tan a mano,
> como el alzar la olla, oler el guiso
> y ver que está en su punto! ¡Si era claro:
> tanta alegría por tan poco costo
> era verdad, era verdad! Ah, cuándo
> me daré cuenta de que todo es simple.
>
>   . . . and it was all
> so simple, all so much on hand,
> like raising the pot, smelling the stew
> and seeing that it is at its point! Why, it was clear:
> so much happiness for so small a price
> was true, was true! Ah, when
> will I realize that everything is simple.

Words like "sencillo," "claro," and "simple" imply a semiotic vision in which there is no longer any distance between the sign and its referent, between appearances and reality. The odor of the stew is a natural sign, one that signifies through its direct, existential connection with the reality that it represents. The poet's innocence, paradoxically, resulted from being too sophisticated for his own good. In his awareness of the duplicity of all signs, he did not realize that appearances can in fact correspond directly to reality.

The poet's return to his city, then, is a return to innocence. A journey in time as well as space, it constitutes an attempt to regain the lost vision of childhood. "A las puertas de la ciudad" is a key poem in the thematic development of *Conjuros*, for it weaves together several metaphors developed independently in other poems. The subsequent lines of "A las puertas" develop intertextual references to several other poems in the book. The poet surrenders his self in the practice of agriculture, as in "El canto de linos" (The song of Flax) (76–77). He is both a cultivator of the earth and, metaphorically, a part of the earth itself. A reference to the river Duero evokes "Al ruido del Duero" (To the Sound of the Duero) (81–82), in which this river symbolizes the purity of the poet's native earth. The central image of "Ante una pared de adobe" (Before an adobe wall) (90), a poem that deals with the unity of man in nature in the practice of agriculture, also appears. "A las puertas de la ciudad" has the same assonantal rhyme pattern as both this poem and "Alto jornal" (High workday) (97), and shares many of the same rhyming words: *pasos, vano, mano, arado, trabajo, amo, salvo.* The image of the river leads to a ritual purification reminiscent of "A mi ropa tendida" (To my hanging clothes). The poet's reintegration into his society takes the form of a ritual cleansing in which the poet purifies himself by rejecting his previous self. The newly washed clothing of "A mi ropa tendida" represents the reborn self who is no longer alienated from his community.

The final lines of "A las puertas de la ciudad" express the poet's return to the city through an agricultural metaphor:

> Perdón si antes no os quise dar la mano
> pero yo qué sabía. Vuelvo alegre
> y esta calma da a mis pasos
> el buen compás, la buena
> marcha hacia la ciudad de mis pecados.
> ¡De par en par las puertas! Voy. Y entro
> tan seguro, tan llano
> como el que barbechó en enero y sabe
> que la tierra no falla, y un buen día
> se va tranquilo a recoger su grano.

(75)

> Forgive me if before I did not want to give you my hand
> but what did I know. I return, happy,
> and this calm gives my steps
> the good beat, the good

march toward the city of my sins.
The gates wide open! I go. And I enter
so sure, so plain
as he who plowed in January and knows
that the earth does not fail, and one good day
leaves calmly to harvest his grain.

Normally we think of the city as the antithesis of the countryside, but here it is identified with a cultivated field: the poet returns to his birthplace as this very idealized farmer comes to harvest his crops.

The analogies developed in "A la respiración en la llanura" and "A la puertas de la ciudad" aim to unite self, community, and nature in a single world. Yet there is a crucial ambiguity in the poet's project. In the first poem in Conjuros the speaker invites his fellow human beings to participate with him in the communion with nature that he has already achieved. In "A las puertas de la ciudad," on the contrary, it is an alienated poet who seeks to rejoin a community which has itself remained in harmony with nature. The protagonist of Conjuros, then, is alternately superior to the people of his city, since he can teach them to regain their connection with the earth and a true sense of their own community, and inferior to them, as an oversophisticated exile who has rejected the innocence and purity of his childhood world. He is a prophet, awakening his people to a new vision of society, but he is also a scapegoat, ejected from his community because of his inability to participate fully in their social solidarity.

A vivid symbol of the poet's alienation is his lameness, his inability to walk in step with the people of the city.[9] In his triumphant homecoming in "A las puertas de la ciudad" the poet sees himself as walking with "el buen compás, la buena / marcha." Yet he is also the social outcast who commits "faux pas." In "El baile de Aguedas" (The dance of the Aguedas), the dancers reject him for his clumsiness, thus excluding him from their communal celebration of social solidarity:

Veo que no queréis bailar conmigo
y hacéis muy bien. Si hasta ahora
no hice más que pisaros, si hasta ahora
no moví al aire vuestro estos pies cojos.

(119)

I see that you do not want to dance with me
and you do very well. Why, until now

I did nothing more than step on you, why, until now
I did not move these lame feet to your air.

Lameness, of course, is the traditional mark of the scapegoat, the
victim who takes upon himself a collective sin and whose sacrifice therefore purifies the community. This figure is ambiguous,
for he is both a sinner and, through his subsequent purification of
society, a savior, even a Christ figure.

In "Dando una vuelta por mi calle" (Taking a walk on my
street) the ambiguity between these two perspectives is especially acute. The form of this poem, with its second thoughts,
self-corrections, and reversals, imitates the poet's indecisive wan-
dering through the city. Addressing his own feet in the opening
lines, the speaker appears divided against himself:

> Basta, pies callejeros,
> no estáis pisando mosto, andad, en marcha.
> ¿Qué hacéis por esta calle,
> aquí, en la calle de mis correrías?

(93)

> Enough, street-roaming feet,
> you are not stepping on must, walk, move.
> What are you doing on this street,
> here, in the street of my forays?

From the perspective outside the gates in "A las puertas de la
ciudad," the poet's reintegration appears a simple affair. Once
inside the city, however, his identification with his community
becomes more complicated. The city no longer appears as a
single, unified whole but rather as a duplicitous, dangerous
world that will betray the poet's innocence. In the lines that
follow the speaker views himself as a trapped, hunted animal.
The exclamation that follows these lines, in a characteristically
abrupt change of tone, appeals once again to the innocence of the
city: "¡Calle mayor de mi esperanza, suenen / en ti los pasos de
mi vida . . . !" [Calle mayor of my hope, let the steps of my life
resound in you] (93). This exalted tone continues for several more
lines. Exclamations occur in virtually every poem in Conjuros.
(They are even more frequent in the original edition of the book;
Rodríguez has eliminated many from subsequent reprintings.) It
is easy to take them as a sign of naive enthusiasm. More often
than not, however, they reveal the speaker's insecurity. In this
poem, the exclamatory tone "protests too much." Carried away

with his agriculture metaphor, the poet demands that the city be kept pure and uncorrupted:

> ¡Alcalde óigame, alcalde,
> que no la asfalten nunca, que no dejen
> pisar por ella más que a los de tierra
> de bien sentado pan y vino moro!

(93)

> Mayor listen to me, mayor,
> let them never pave it, allow
> to walk there only those of the land
> of well-settled bread and moorish wine!

At this moment of enthusiasm for the purity of his rural community the poet turns back on himself, realizing that he would not qualify under his own definition of innocence. The remainder of the poem strikes a more sober note, as the poet sees himself once again as an impure, lame outsider:

> Perdón, que por la calle va quien quiere
> y yo no debo hablar así. Qué multa
> me pondrían a mí, a mí el primero,
> si me vieran lo cojo,
> lo maleante que ando desde entonces.
> Alto, alto mis pasos.
> . . . .
> Los que estáis ahí, al sol, echadme, echadme.

(93–94)

> Sorry, for anyone who wants can walk the street
> and I should not speak like this. What a fine
> they would assess me, me first of all,
> if they saw how lame,
> how perversely I walk since then.
> Halt, halt my steps.
> . . . .
> You who are there, in the sun, throw me out, throw me out.

The poet is an ideal scapegoat because of his ambiguous position in the community. He belongs to and identifies with this community, yet his lameness sets him apart. In order to return as an undifferentiated member of his society, his heart must beat in step with his fellow citizens:

> Ya volveré yo cuando
> se me acompase el corazón con estos

pasos a los que invoco,
a los que estoy oyendo hoy por la tarde
sonar en esta acera,
en esta callejón que da a la vida.

(94)

I will return when
my heart is synchronized with these
steps which I invoke,
those that I am hearing this afternoon
sounding on this sidewalk,
on this alleyway that leads to life.

The uncertainty of the poet's status results from an inherent ambiguity in the idea of "social poetry" itself. Socially conscious writers must reconcile two conflicting visions of society, the idealized "pueblo" that they claim to represent and the real society in all of its contradictions. They must simultaneously identify with an ideal community and maintain a critical distance from a potentially corrupt social order. The poet of *Conjuros* appears alternatively as an oversophisticated exile, returning to his birthplace in order to regain his lost innocence, and as a prophet of social solidarity. The danger inherent in the first alternative is that the poet will be rejected because of his impurity, his difference from the common man. The attempt to dissolve this difference is futile, for it is inseparable from his very status as a poet. Addressing the problem of proletarian art, William Empson observed that "to produce pure proletarian art the artist must be at one with the worker; this is impossible, not for political reasons, but because the artist is never at one with any public."[10] In *Conjuros* the poet's separation from his audience is not merely a question of social class but is inherent in his very use of language. Since the poet's original alienation from society is inseparable from his linguistic awakening, he cannot overcome this alienation without renouncing his art.

Even if a total identification between poet and audience were possible, it would not be desirable, for the poet speaks as a prophet of a social vision that the audience itself does not yet fully possess. While appearing merely to reflect the consciousness of the common people, the social poet actually creates this consciousness through the poetic word. As we shall see later, this privileged position as the creator of a social vision has even more serious consequences than does the poet's alienation, for it implies that the community itself may be corrupt. The poet must preach to the people of his city because they have lost the true basis of their own solidarity.

The poet of *Conjuros* appears to reject the mediation of language, to rediscover the innocent signs that signify through their direct connection to reality. At the same time, his attempt to integrate himself into his community depends on the mediation of figurative language. The contradictions involved in the poet's attempt at social solidarity become increasingly evident as the metaphorical system of *Conjuros* develops throughout the volume. Metaphor, with its capacity to dissolve differences, seems ideally suited to the project of identification: to equate a city with a field of grain is to elide all the aspects in which the city is most *unlike* the field. Yet figurative language, as Barthes notes in a different context, is potentially divisive:

> We ordinarily believe that the literary effort consists in seeking out affinities, correspondences, similitudes, and that the writer's function is *to unite* man and Nature in a single world. . . . Yet metaphor, a fundamental figure of literature, can also be understood as a powerful instrument of disjunction.[11]

These two aspects of rhetoric, I would add, are virtually inseparable: in order to unify disparate worlds language must stand between them and thus keep them apart. It is not so much that some metaphors unify and others divide, but that figurative language is inherently both unifying and disjunctive.

In the poems of *Conjuros* the contrast between these two opposing functions of figurative language is especially acute. It is interesting to observe that while thematic summaries of the book tend to stress the unity of the poet's world, stylistic analyses uncover a disjunctive technique. The single aspect of Rodríguez's poetry that has attracted the most serious critical attention is the tension between the literal and figurative planes of meaning of his many extended comparisons. Carlos Bousoño focuses on this problem in one of the first significant essays on the poet: the originality of Rodríguez's work is to be found in his use of "disemic allegory," or "metaphorical realism." In a normal allegory or a "traditional metaphor," the figurative meaning displaces the literal sense of the words. In Rodríguez's poems, on the other hand, the literal level continues to function autonomously. The realistic depiction of rural life is not merely an allegory for other, more transcendent themes. Rather, the poet interprets this ordinary reality in transcendent terms without ever losing sight of its concreteness.[12]

Several other critics have explored the implications of the tension between realism and allegory in Rodríguez's work. Andrew P. Debicki recasts Bousoño's observations in terms of the response of a hypothetical reader, who will be disconcerted by the switches from one "code" to another, usually from a description of an ordinary event to its symbolic interpretation.[13] Philip Silver analyzes Rodríguez's figurative language in terms of "automatism," the process by which the two planes of a metaphorical system begin to develop autonomously from each other through a series of irrational associations. "A partir de *Conjuros*," writes Silver, "lo característico de la obra de Rodríguez es la aparición de un tipo de poema enhebrado en una o varias metáforas continuadas de corte rimbaudiano, en que la 'arbitrariedad' del sistema metafórico tiende a trastornar su carácter referencial." [Beginning with *Conjuros* the must characteristic aspect of Rodríguez's work is the appearance of a type of poem which is threaded on one or several continuous metaphors of the Rimbaldian type, in which the "arbitrariness" of the metaphoric system tends to disturb its referential character.][14]

Bousoño considers the use of "disemic allegory" to be unique to the author of *Conjuros*. Debicki and Silver also imply that this metaphorical technique is what makes his work original. Without disputing Rodríguez's originality, it would perhaps be more accurate to say that his poetry foregrounds the tension between the literal and figurative planes of meaning (or between the divisive and unifying functions of metaphor) that is implicit in any use of figurative language.[15] Paradoxically, the greater the emphasis on the absolute identity of literal and figurative meaning, the more the differences between them will become evident. In his use of metaphor to unite potentially disparate worlds, Rodríguez runs the risk of exposing this very disparity.

The rhetorical force of Rodríguez's central metaphor depends upon an implicit metonymy: the social order resembles the natural order insofar as it maintains its direct connection with it. The landscape in "A la respiración en la llanura," for example, is a metaphor for a human community, but it is above all the scene where the act of communion with nature takes place. The city in "A las puertas de la ciudad" resembles a field of grain but also lies next to the field: it is a community based on the practice of agriculture. The natural solidarity of this community, then, depends on its direct, existential connection to nature. It is this confusion of resemblance and contiguity that allows the poet to achieve his fusion of the social and natural orders and his simultaneous integration into his community. Identifying the city with the countryside around it, he envisions an authentic social order based on the natural world itself. This dependence on relations of contiguity also means, however, that the idea of a natural social order is falsifiable. Unlike metaphor, which claims to express an essential correspondence between two realities, metonymy relies on a more fortuitous, accidental link. "To maintain the primacy of metaphor," writes Culler, "is to treat language as a device for the expression of thoughts, perceptions, truth. To posit the dependency of metaphor on metonymy is to treat what language expresses as the effect of contingent, conventional relations and a system of mechanical processes."[16]

The fortuitousness of metonymy is evident in the associative process by which a metaphorical system gains its autonomy. As Silver explains, the two planes of Rodríguez's extended comparisons develop through chance associations and plays on words. As it becomes increasingly difficult to relate the elements of one plane to those in the other, the metaphor reveals the separation between the two realities that it had attempted to unite. The process that Silver describes is most evident in several poems of the fourth and final section of *Conjuros*. These poems often follow an "Icarus" pattern: a metaphorical system develops, gains autonomy, and eventually reaches its breaking point, returning once again to the earth. This pattern is evident in the rhetorical tone of the poems: an increasingly exalted exclamation leading to a final moment of dejection.[17] Images of flight and descent are also frequent. The poet's effort to gain transcendence stands opposed to his downward trajectory toward the earth. "Incidente en los Jerónimos" concerns the unsuccessful flight of a jackdaw, who is also the speaker of the poem. In the final lines the implicit comparison between the bird's flight and the poet's attempt to join his society becomes explicit:

> Llegaré. Llegaré. ¡Ahí está mi vida,
> ahí está el altar, ahí brilla mi pueblo!
> Un poco más. Ya casi. . .
>
> . . . .
> Así, así . . . Ya, ya . . . ¡Qué mala suerte!
> ¡Ya por tan poco! Un grajo, un hombre a tierra.[18]
>
> I will arrive. I will arrive. There is my life,
> there is the altar, there shines my people!
> A little more. Now almost . . .
>
> . . . .
> Like this, like this . . . now, now . . . What bad luck!
> Failing by so little! A jackdaw, a man on the earth.

A similar effect occurs in "Caza mayor," in which the poet's bed is compared to the earth. As in "Inicidente," this comparison becomes explicit only in the final lines, in which the bed is equated with a grave.

The raveling and unraveling of a metaphorical system is most evident in "Visión a la hora de siesta" (Vision at the hour of the siesta), the poem that opens "Libro cuarto." As the speaker's sister sews, a ray of light enters through the window and transforms her into a stitch in the larger fabric of the world:

> ¡Si esa es mi hermana y cose cuarto adentro
> tan tranquila y, de pronto,
> ¡quitadla!, la da el sol y un simple rayo
> la enhebra, y en él queda bien zurcida,
> puntada blanca de la luz del mundo!

(107)

> Why this is my sister and she is sewing inside
> so calm and suddenly
> take her away! the sun touches here and a simple ray
> threads her, and on it she becomes well-mended,
> a white stitch of the world's light!

From a single metaphor the poet weaves others in rapid succession. The light becomes yeast that ferments human solidarity, then once again the thread or yarn that connects everything in the world together:

> Y,¡cerrad las ventanas!, ese rayo,
> eterna levadura, se nos echa
> encima, y nos fermenta, y en él cuaja
> nuestro amasado corazón y, como
> la insurrección de un pueblo,
> se extiende, avanza y cubre
> toda la tierra ya, teje y desteje
> la estopa hostil del hombre y allí, a una,
> en el mesón del tiempo, siempre caro,
> allí, a la puerta, en el telar hermoso,
> vamos tejiendo, urdiendo
> la camisa de Dios, el limpio sayo
> de la vida y la muerte.

> And, close the windows!, that ray,
> eternal yeast, jumps
> on top of us, and ferments us, and in it
> our kneaded heart takes form and, like

                the insurrection of a people,
                it extends, advances and covers
                the entire earth already, weaves and unweaves
                the hostile burlap of man and there, at one,
                in the inn of time, always expensive,
                there, at the door, in its beautiful fabric,
                we go along weaving, fashioning
                God's shirt, the clean apron
                of life and death.

The phrase, "insurrección de un pueblo," is not innocent in the
context of postwar Spanish poetry. In relation to the project of
Conjuros, more specifically, this line points to the relation between metaphorical elaboration and social solidarity: the social
function of the poet is to join human beings together through
figurative language. Up until this point in the poem the speaker's
tone has become increasingly more exalted, his vision more
grandiose. Near the halfway point, however, he stops himself and
describes the dissolution of his metaphorical system. No sooner
is the process of weaving complete than the entire fabric of his
creation begins to come undone:

                Pero, ¿ahora,
                qué pasa?: cuando estaba
                viendo colgar del cielo
                la bandera inmortal, como en los días
                de fiesta en mi ciudad cuelga la enseña
                roja y gualda, oídme, cuando
                veía ese inmenso lienzo en el que cada
                ligera trama es una vida entera
                ocupar el espacio,
                he aquí que un aliento, un tenue oreo,
                después una voz clara
                se alza, y con tal temple,
                con tal metal esa voz suena ahora
                que hilo a hilo cantando se descose
                una vida, otra, otra,
                de aquel gran sayo, y se oye como un himno,
                escuchad, y de pronto . . .

                De pronto estoy despierto y es día

                                                    (107–8)

                But now
                what's happening?: as I was

seeing the immortal flag
hang from the sky, as on holidays
in my city they hang the red and yellow
banner, listen to me, as
I saw that immense canvas, in which each
light plot is a whole life,
occupy space,
behold a breath, a tenuous stream,
then a clear voice
arises, and with such a timbre,
with such a metal this voice sounds now
that thread by thread singing
one life, another, another, comes unsewn
of that great apron, and something like a hymn is heard,
listen, and suddenly . . .

Suddenly I am awake and it is day.

The culminating moment of the poet's vision, when he sees the
flag or fabric fill the entire universe and include every individual
life, is also the moment of its greatest precariousness. The most
tenuous breath is sufficient to begin the process of dissolution. If,
as Barthes has explained, a text is the weaving together of different codes, Rodríguez's text literally begins to come unraveled
at this point.[19] In a manner of speaking, the poet "loses the
thread" and awakens once again to the ordinary reality with
which his vision began.

The pattern of the successive elaboration and crisis of a metaphor—the raveling and unraveling of the text—observed in "Visión a la hora de la siesta" and other poems in the final section of
Conjuros occurs, on a larger scale, throughout the volume as a
whole. The central metaphor of the work is the comparison
between the unity of the natural world and the solidarity of the
social order. As these potentially disparate systems develop independently of each other, they threaten to expose once again the
two parallel gaps, between poet and society and between society
and nature, that this metaphor was originally designed to close.
The separate "codes"—to employ Debicki's term—of the natural
and the social orders come into direct conflict with each other.
As Debicki points out, the disparity between two parallel codes
can cause surprise and even humor.[20] The disjunction between
nature and society ultimately has a more serious consequence,
bringing about the impasse of the project of identification and the
poet's final disillusionment.[21]

The last poem in *Conjuros*, "Pinar amanecido" (Pine grove at dawn), is a counterpart to "A las puertas de la ciudad," the poem from the first section that best exemplifies the unity of society and nature. Once again the solidarity of a community finds representation to a natural metaphor: the grove of pines, like the field of grain in the earlier poem, is a metaphor for the city. The traveler whom the speaker addresses throughout is a double for the poet himself:

> Viajero, tú nunca
> te olvidarás, si pisas estas tierras
> del pino. Cuánta salud, cuánto aire
> limpio nos da. No sientes
> junto al pinar la cura,
> el claro respirar del pulmón nuevo,
> el fresco riego de la vida? Eso
> es lo que importa ¡Pino piñonero,
> que llegue a la ciudad y sólo vea
> la cercanía hermosa
> del hombre! ¡Todos juntos,
> pared contra pared, todos del brazo
> por las calles
> esperando las bodas
> de corazón!

(121)

> Traveler, you never
> will forget, if you walk these lands
> the pine. How much health, how much clean
> air it gives us. Do you not feel
> near the pine grove the cure,
> the clear breathing of the new lung,
> the fresh watering of life? This
> is what matters. Edible pine,
> let it reach the city and only see
> the beautiful closeness
> of man! All together,
> wall against wall, all arm in arm
> through the streets
> awaiting the wedding
> of the heart!

The "pinar" of the opening lines seems quite literal. Thus the apparent shift of scene from pine grove to city in the ninth line is momentarily disconcerting. The "viajero," humorously enough, becomes a "pino piñonero." The reason behind the unconventional equation of the rural and the urban soon becomes evident, as the poet is caught up in an optimistic vision of social solidarity:

> ¡Todos cogidos de la mano, todos
> cogidos de la vida
> en torno
> de la humildad del hombre!
> Ah, solidaridad. Ah, tú paloma
> madre: mete el buen pico,
> mete el buen grano hermoso
> hasta la buche a tus crías.

> All holding hands, all
> holding lives
> around
> the humbleness of man!
> Ah, solidarity. Ah, you mother
> dove: stick in your good beak,
> stick the good, beautiful grain
> into the mouths of your young.

The model for human solidarity is the natural bond between the mother bird and her young.

Up until this point in the poem there has been no hint of irony. The speaker's exalted tone corresponds to what the critics have called the youthful, unreflective voice of Rodríguez's early poetry. At the same time the very exaggeration of tone warns the reader of a coming fall. The over-use of rather vague adjectives, especially "bueno" and "hermoso," seems uncharacteristic of Rodríguez's talent at its best. In the next section of the poem the mood becomes slightly more subdued:

> Y ahora, viajero,
> al cantar por segunda vez el gallo,
> ve al pinar y allí espérame.
> . . . .
> tronco a tronco, hombre a hombre,
> ciudad, pinar, cantemos:
> que el amor nos ha unido
> pino por pino, casa
> por casa.

$$(121-22)$$

> And now, traveler,
> when you hear the cock crow a second time

go to the pine grove and wait for me there.

. . . .

trunk by trunk, man by man,
city, pine grove, let us sing:
that love has linked us
pine to pine, house
to house.

In contrast to the beginning of the poem, the affirmation of
solidarity is no longer a spontaneous celebration. It has become
instead a conscious act of will. The reference to the cock crowing
twice, a possible allusion to Peter's denial of Jesus in the New
Testament (Mark 14:30), adds an ominous note. In the abrupt
revelation in the following lines the poet acknowledges that he
too is denying the truth:

Nunca digamos la verdad en esta
sagrada hora del día.
Pobre de aquel que mire
y vea claro, vea
entrar a saco en el pinar la inmensa
justicia de la luz, esté en el sitio
que a la ciudad ha puesto la audaz horda
de las estrellas, la implacable hueste
del espacio.

(122)

Let us never tell the truth in this
sacred hour of the day.
Poor is he who looks
and sees clear, sees
entering the pine grove to plunder the immense
justice of light, who is in the city
that is besieged by the audacious horde
of the stars, the implacable host
of space.

While recognizing the falsity of his optimistic vision, the poet
still prefers an illusory social solidarity to the terrible truth.
Words that ordinarily have positive connotations—*verdad, justicia, luz, espacio*—take on a negative force. This irony is double-
edged, however, for the poet reveals the very truth that he appears to want to deny, that his community is based on fear:

Pobre de aquel que vea
que lo que une es la defensa, el miedo.

¡Un paso al frente el que ose
mirar la faz de la pureza, alzarle
la infantil falda casta
a la alegría!
Qué sutil añagaza, ruin chanchullo,
bien adobado cebo
de la apariencia.

Poor is he who sees
that what unites is defense, fear.
One step forward he who dares
to looks at the face of purity, lift up
the chaste, childlike skirt
of happiness!
What a subtle trap, a ruinous fraud,
a well-worked bait
of appearance.

The poet views the appearance of innocence as a seductive trap.
This attitude is an inversion of the simple theory of the sign put
forward in "A la puertas de la ciudad," according to which such
appearances correspond to the truth. Reality is essentially deceptive: to reach the truth one must see beyond it. To participate
directly in this illusory web of signs is to lose one's capacity for
vision.

In spite of the distrustful vision of the sign articulated in these
lines, the poet continues to shy away from the force of his
revelation. In a paradox similar to the negative vision of the light
in *Don de la ebriedad*, in which the poet denies the existence of
the very vision he is creating through his poem, the speaker of
"Pinar amanecido" protests against a truth that he alone has
uncovered. The final lines of the poem present this paradox in its
most extreme form, as the poet simultaneously lays bear the
negative truth about his society and attempts to return to his
optimistic vision:

¿Dónde el amor, dónde el valor, sí, dónde
la compañía? Viajero,
sigue cantando la amistad dichosa
en el pinar amaneciente. Nunca
creas esto que he dicho:
canta y canta. Tú, nunca
digas por estas tierras
que hay poco amor y mucho miedo siempre.

> Where is love, courage, yes, where
> is company? Traveler,
> continue singing to fortunate friendship
> in the dawning pine grove. Never
> believe what I have said:
> sing and sing. You, never
> say that in these lands
> there is little love and much fear always.

This final sentence, which concludes both "Pinar amanecido" and *Conjuros*, unmasks the illusion of social solidarity that has sustained the poet's enterprise throughout the volume. Silver quotes these lines in order to dissociate Rodríguez completely from social poetry. "Esta sentencia abrumadora, bastante subversiva, da la justa medida de lo poco que tiene que ver la poesía de Rodríguez con la llamada 'social'" [This devastating judgement, rather subversive, provides an accurate measure of the little that Rodríguez's poetry has to do with the poetry called "social"].[22] As a statement about *Conjuros* or about Rodríguez's poetry as a whole, this observation is an oversimplification. Silver is correct, however, in noting the subversive force of the conclusion. The poet of *Conjuros* has exposed a central fiction of social poetry: the solidarity of an ideal community.

The poet's failure to attain a true social solidarity with the people of his city is also a failure of language. Appearing to deny the linguistic nature of his enterprise, he attempts to participate in his community through the mediation of poetic language. This participation is doomed, however, by its own rhetorical nature. As the metaphorical system of *Conjuros* becomes more complex, its inherent contradictions become more apparent. The comparisons that promised to link human beings and nature in a single harmonious whole collapse under their own weight, revealing the differences that separate the poet from a society that is itself alienated from the world.

The attitude toward language suggested in the final lines of *Conjuros* echoes the visionary poetics that the poet had earlier rejected in *Don de la ebriedad*; the poet stands apart from a world of deceptive appearances and reveals the truth through his mastery of a duplicitous poetic language. In his rediscovery of the arbirariness of the sign, Rodríguez has come full circle. What differentiates the poet's new position from his previous one is his new understanding of the ethical value of poetic language. The conclusion of *Conjuros* does not lead back to the alienated poetic of transcendent vision but rather toward the more critical vision of society to be articulated in *Alianza y condena* (1965). The vision of the sign implicit in "Pinar amanecido" and further explored in Rodríguez's subsequent book corresponds to a new idea of the poet's social function: rather than identifying completely with his community, the poet must maintain a critical distance in order to denounce the falsity and corruption of the social order.

4

Alianza y Condena: The Dialectic of the Sign

> Dentro de la alianza existe la condena, igual que dentro de la condena existe la alianza. Es un proceso (para decirlo con una palabra muy cursi) dialéctico.
>
> Within alliance there is condemnation, just as within condemnation there is alliance. It is a *dialectical* process (to say it with a very vulgar word).
>
> —Claudio Rodríguez

"Pinar amanecido," the final poem of *Conjuros*, poses a dilemma that is at once semiotic and ethical: an uncritical participation in the world, made possible by the ideal of a "natural" language, leads to self-deception, while a more skeptical view of the sign produces alienation from the community. The speaker's desire to preserve his illusion at the end of this poem implies that the self-surrender that is the basis of his engagement with reality is incompatible with a critical vision of the truth. It is this dilemma that Rodríguez explores in *Alianza y condena* (Alliance and condemnation) (1965), his most complete and explicit meditation on the sign. *Alianza* resembles *Don de la ebriedad* in its more direct concern with the problems of language. It is Rodríguez's most explicitly metapoetic work. As in the first collection the poet-protagonist attempts to overcome the duplicity of the linguistic sign in order to integrate himself once more into the world. The most significant difference, however, is that in the later book the poet's consciousness of the arbitrariness of the sign is irrevocable: he no longer attempts to attain a state of linguistic unconsciousness. The more innocent vision of reality to which he returns, then, is ultimately a paradoxical one.

The task facing the poet-protagonist of *Alianza y condena* is to reconcile language with the world, but without sacrificing his critical vision of both language and reality. In his attempt to resolve this dilemma he explores the ambiguities inherent in the notion of the arbitrariness of the sign. Usually this arbitrariness is viewed in negative terms, since it is linked to the inherent deceptiveness of language. In spite of its deceptive nature, however, language can also reveal the truth: its capacity to deceive, in fact, is inseparable from its capacity to unmask deceit. This apparent contradiction results from the fact that an awareness that words do not always coincide with things is necessary before one can call into question language's representation of reality.

Another theoretical construct that Rodríguez examines in these poems is the very nature of the truth that lies behind language. Rodríguez views this "truth" as a duplicitous sign in its own right. The unmasking of illusions that the poet practices in several poems reveals a negative, destructive reality. Nevertheless, this reality might also conceal another, more positive truth. Rather than a simple relation between a deceptive sign and the truth it conceals, Rodríguez posits several layers of signs, each of which must be interpreted in its turn. We might conceive of the potentially positive working of language as a significant exception to a predominately negative view of language. The idea that language is normally but not necessarily deceptive allows the poet to go beyond his critical vision and develop a more complete vision of the sign. A series of dialectical transformations of language leads to the rediscovery of innocence.[1] This innocence, however, reveals a consciousness of its own fictionality: the poet remains fully aware that language is arbitrary, that it can only coincide with the truth in rare, exceptional moments of vision.[2]

Alianza y condena not only marks a culminating moment in Rodríguez's own development as a writer but also exemplifies a broader tendency in Spanish poetry of the 1960s toward a rigorously self-conscious concern with the ethical dimension of poetic language. Whereas the metapoetic commentary of *Don de la ebriedad* was anomalous and even unintelligible in the context of the social poetry of the early fifties, the search for an authentic language that stands at the center of *Alianza* is the common preoccupation of many Spanish poets of the following decade. For writers such as José Angel Valente, Angel González, and Jaime Gil de Biedma, the social fabric of postwar Spain is based on a lie; language, along with other social conventions, serves primarily to conceal the truth. A common motif in Spanish poetry of the period is the idea that words have been so debased by their use as official discourse and propaganda that they have lost their capacity to represent the truth.[3]

The younger poets' critique of a decadent and deceptive language is a variation and reversal of what Gustav Siebenmann has identified as one the commonplaces of social poetry: "la denuncia de la vacua palabra literaria" [the denunciation of the vacuous literary word].[4] Whereas the social poets denounce the empty language of uncommitted, "dehumanized" poetry, Rodríguez's contemporaries extend their criticism of false language to the rhetoric of social poetry itself. Rodríguez speaks of

> Compañeros
> falsos y taciturnos,
> cebados de consignas, si tan ricos
> de propaganda, de canción tan pobres.[5]

> False and taciturn
> companions,
> fattened with party lines, if so rich
> in propaganda, in song so poor.

This passage draws a clear link between linguistic duplicity, ideological dogmatism, and poetic sterility. Although this critique applies equally well to the official language of the Franco regime, in this case it refers primarily to the misuse of language on the left, as is evident in the use of such words as "compañeros" and "consignas." The poetics of social poetry emphasize the ideal of a simple, transparent language: in order to regain a more authentic speech the poet has only to renounce the literary artifice that separates poetry from the masses. We can see this aim even in some of the poems of Rodríguez's own *Conjuros*. Implicit in the critical vision of the poetry of the sixties, in contrast, is an awareness of the more essential difficulty of reconciling language with the truth, even for the poet committed to social justice. Rodríguez and his contemporaries even criticize their own language: José Angel Valente, for example, accuses himself of being "culpable / de las mismas palabras que combato" [guilty / of the same words that I combat].[6] This is an important point, for the younger generation of Spanish poets— those who came of age after 1968—have often claimed that this critique of the inauthentic language of the social poets is their own invention. These poets, often termed the "Novísimos" after Castellet's famous anthology, have attempted to collapse the distinction between the socially concerned poetry of Blas de Otero and Gabriel Celaya, and the more language-conscious work of Rodríguez, Valente, and their contemporaries.[7]

The shift from "poesía social" to "poesía crítica" in postwar Spain can be seen in the difference between *Conjuros* and *Alianza y condena*. Whereas in the earlier book the poet-protagonist strives to identify his voice with that of the community, in *Alianza* he maintains a critical distance from which to observe the falsity of Spanish society. This distance is literal as well as figurative: it is significant that Rodríguez composed the poems of *Alianza* during his years of exile in England. As he writes in one poem, "No podré habitarte, / ciudad cercana. Siempre seré huésped, / nunca vecino" [I will never inhabit you, / nearby city. / I will always be a guest, / never a neighbor](140).

For the critical poet, the language of everyday social life is a series of euphemisms that mask the true nature of things. At the simplest level, the poet's task is to substitute more accurate names for these deceptive labels:

> Jamás casas: barracas,
> jamás calles: trincheras,
> jamás jornal: soldada.
>
> (163–64)

> Never houses: barracks,
> never streets: trenches,
> never a workman's wage: a soldier's.

This denunciation of false language exposes a society that is based on a lie. The juxtaposition of the vast Castilian landscape and the decadence and corruption of Spain in this poem, "Ciudad de meseta" (City on the plain), is reminiscent of Machado's *Campos de Castilla* and other works of the "Generation of '98." (Several previous critics, including José Luis Cano, have already noted this kinship.) "Por tierra de lobos" (In a land of wolves) similarly, is critical in a very harsh and explicit way, denouncing the church and all others who make life "negotiable" (141). Such direct denunciation, however, is uncharacteristic of Rodríguez's poetry. In "Brujas a mediodía" (Witches at noon), the poem that stands at the head of *Alianza y condena*, the poet submerges himself in a world of duplicitous signs with little possibility of distinguishing truth from falsehood:

> No son cosas de viejas,
> ni de agujas sin ojo o alfileres
> sin cabeza. No salta,
> como sal en la lumbre, este sencillo

sortilegio, este viejo
maleficio. Ni hisopo
para rociar ni vela
de cera virgen necesita.

(127)

They are not things of old women,
nor of eyeless needles or headless
pins. It does not jump,
like salt in the light, this simple
spell, this old
curse. It needs neither a hyssop
to sprinkle nor a candle
of virgin wax.

These first lines, which dissociate the witches from their traditional trappings, indicate the metaphorical nature of the title.
The "witchcraft" here is not the conventional nocturnal sorcery
but the seemingly more mundane mysteries of everday reality
that the poet must confront in his search for knowledge: the
subtitle of the poem is "(Hacia el conocimiento)" (Toward
knowledge). This metaphorical technique is typical of
Rodríguez's metapoetry. Rather than directly invoking "words" or
"signs," the poet employs concrete examples of the signifying
process. This allegorical mode of self-consciousness, which contrasts with the more explicit concern with language of a poet like
José Angel Valente, has led critics to underestimate Rodríguez's
theoretical sophistication.[8] The advantage of this technique,
however, is that the poet's meditation on language becomes an
exploration of the nature of reality as well. The concrete objects
of the world become metaphors for language. From another perspective, language itself could be said to be a metaphor for the
process of perceiving reality.

The following lines explain the central metaphor in terms of
the deceitfulness of the sensorial world, subtly reintroducing the
negative connotations of witchcraft that had earlier been dis-
missed:

Cada
forma de vida tiene
un punto de cocción, un meteoro
de burbujas.
. . . . . .
No es sólo el cuerpo,
con su leyenda de torpeza, lo que

nos engaña: en la misma
constitución de la materia, en tanta
claridad que es estafa,
guiños, mejunjes, trémulo
carmín, nos trastornaban. Y huele
a toca negra y aceitosa, a pura
bruja este mediodía de setiembre;
y en los pliegues del aire;
en los altares del espacio, hay vicios
enterrados, lugares
donde se compra el corazón, siniestras
recetas para amores.

(127–128)

                    Each
form of life has
a boiling point, a meteor
of bubbles.

. . . . . .
It is not only the body,
with its legend of clumsiness, that
deceives us: in the very
constitution of matter, in so much
clarity that it is fraud,
winks, potions, tremulous
crimson, disturbed us. And this September noon
smells of a black and oily headdress;
and in the folds of the air,
in the altars of space, there are buried
vices, places
where the heart is bought, sinister
recipes for love.

Michael Mudrovic claims to detect a "sarcastic irony" in this first section of "Brujas." The condemnation of the illusory nature of material reality, however, is explicit rather than ironical. The irony, if anything, is that the poet still finds some attraction in such an explicitly sinister world.[9] In spite of the denunciation of false illusions, reminiscent of "Pinar amanecido" (122), the enchantment of the witches represents the poet's only hope either of participating in the world or of reaching the truth.

The second section of the poem marks a subtle change of tone from the first. The poet's still views reality suspiciously, but his language becomes increasingly ambivalent as he searches for meaning in the deceptive images of the material world. Using a technique similar to that of the first lines of the poem, he contrasts the traditional ingredients of a witches' stew to the more profound enchantment of everyday life.

> todo lo que es cosa de brujas, cosa
> natural, hoy no es nada
> junto a este aquelarre de imágenes que, ahora,
> cuando los seres dejan poca sombra,
> da un reflejo: la vida.
> La vida no es un reflejo
> pero, ¿cuál es su imagen?
>
> (128–29)

> All that is a witches' thing, a natural
> thing, today is nothing
> next to this witches' Sabbath of images that, now,
> when beings leave little shadow,
> gives a reflection: life.
> Life is not a reflection
> but what is its image?

The game of mirrors in this passage produces an effect of confusion. Life appears as the *reflection* of an *image*; it is thus at two removes from a more essential reality, barely glimpsed, perhaps, in the small shadows of "los seres." The last two lines here reverse this perspective: "life" is no longer a representation but reality itself. As in "Las imágenes" from *Don de la ebriedad*, the problem becomes one of distinguishing the truth from its myriad images.

The series of rhetorical questions that follows reveals an even more ambivalent attitude toward the nature of knowledge, culminating in the central dilemma of whether it is preferable to preserve a comforting facade or to confront the truth head-on:

> ¿Por qué quien ama nunca
> busca verdad, sino que busca dicha?
> ¿Cómo sin la verdad
> puede existir la dicha? He aquí todo.
>
> (129)

> Why does he who loves never
> seek truth, but seeks happiness?
> How without truth
> can happiness exist? This is everything.

These lines echo the paradox of "Pinar amanecido," in which the speaker implores his alter ego to continue to live a lie rather than to face the destructive truth: "Nunca digas la verdad" [Never tell the truth] (122). The injunction "do not believe what I am saying," however, is by definition impossible to obey. To acknowledge the contradiction between truth and happiness is already to privilege the truth, for the dilemma only exists once the illusion has been exposed.

The concluding lines of "Brujas a mediodía" make it clear that the poet cannot remain apart from the material world, even as he recognizes it as a web of illusions:

> Y ahora
> a mediodía
> si ellas nos besan desde tantas cosas,
> ¿dónde estará su noche,
> dónde sus labios, dónde nuestra boca
> para aceptar tanta mentira y tanto
> amor?
>
> (130)

> And now
> at noon,
> if they kiss us from so many things,
> where will their night be,
> where their lips, where our mouth
> to accept so many lies and so much
> love?

The poet distrusts reality, but his suspicions do not lead him to an attitude of detachment. In his effort to strip away illusions he must engage reality in all of its deceptiveness. It is no longer possible simply to deny the deceptive nature of reality, living an illusory existence. Nor can the poet remain detached from these illusions, in a timeless world created by language (as in the visionary poetics of *Don de la ebriedad*). The unanswerable rhetorical questions with which he ends this poem exemplify the poet's fundamentally ambivalent attitude toward the deceptive signs of the world.[10]

The poet's predicament, then, is to be caught between two unacceptable alternatives, an illusory language and a disillusionment that is purely negative. The first lines of "Cáscaras" compare language to other things that protect us by concealing the truth. There is an oblique illusion to the classical myth of Semele, who is destroyed when Zeus reveals himself to her in his undisguised form:

> El nombre de las cosas, que es mentira
> y es caridad, el traje

> que cubre el cuerpo amado
> para que no muramos por la calle
> ante él . . .
> la cautela del sobre, que protege
> traición o amor, dinero o trampa,
> la inmensa cicatriz que oculta la honda herida,
> son nuestro ruin amparo.
>
> (136)

> The names of things, that are a lie
> and are charity, the clothes
> that cover the beloved body
> so that we don't die in the street
> before it . . .
> the caution of the envelope, which protects
> betrayal or love, money or a trick,
> the immense scar that hides the deep wound,
> are our despicable protection.

Each of the metaphors for the sign in this passage reveals the double nature of language as "mentira" and "caridad." Social conventions are signs that guard us against "la verdad que mata" [the truth that kills] (136), but their protection is ultimately harmful. "Cáscaras," like "Brujas a mediodía," is divided into two sections. The first section of each poem presents a bleak view of both language and reality that underlies it, while the second section emphasizes the necessity of engaging with the world all the same. In contrast to the half-hearted appeal to illusion in "Pinar amanecido," the final lines of "Cáscaras" command the implied reader to continue to search for the truth:

> muerde la dura cáscara,
> muerde aunque nunca llegues
> hasta la celda donde cuaja la fruta.
>
> (138)

> bite the hard husk
> bite although you never arrive
> at the cell where the fruit is formed.

In "Nieve en la noche" (Snow in the night), a poem from the second section of *Alianza*, the insistence on the necessity of stripping away illusions is even stronger. This poem reverses the central image of *Don de la ebriedad*. The critical poet of *Alianza y condena*, like the visionary of *Don de la ebriedad*, attempts to see beyond the deceptiveness of the world, to unmask the truth hidden behind false appearances. The difference is that this truth is now a negative one: the sign is no longer a night that conceals the light of day, but rather a false day that conceals a destructive night. In the first lines of the poem the snow disguises the unpleasantness of reality:

> Yo quiero ver qué arrugas
> oculta esta doncella
> máscara, qué ruin tiña,
> qué feroz epidemia
> cela el rostro inocente
> de cada copo.

(159)

> I want to see what wrinkles
> this damsel mask
> conceals, what despicable dye,
> what ferocious epidemic
> hides the innocent face
> of each flake.

The motif of cosmetics, a mask covering a woman's wrinkles, is a frequent one in baroque poetry. As in the baroque this metaphor serves to underscore the deceptiveness of surface beauty. The deception here is double: the snow conceals not only the ugly reality underneath it but also its own nature as a "ruin tiña." Rodríguez's language has a baroque complexity: the snow, already a metaphor for the sign, is described in turn by a series of other metaphors, a technique described by Siebenmann as "la metáfora previa metaforizada a su vez" [a prior metaphor which in turn is metaphorized].[11] It becomes plaster, the day, a scar on the face of the earth, and finally the lime that is used to whitewash houses:

> Escenas
> sin vanidad, se cubren
> con andamiajes, trémulas
> escayolas, molduras
> de un instante. Es la feria
> de la mentira: ahora
> es mediodía en plena
> noche, y se cicatriza
> la eterna herida abierta
> de la tierra, y las casas

lucen con la cal nueva
que revoca sus pobres
fachadas verdaderas.

                    Scenes
without vanity are covered
with scaffolding, tremulous
plaster, molds
of an instant. It is the fair
of the lie: now it is noon
at full night, and the eternal
open wound of earth
is scarred over. And the houses
shine with the new lime
that whitewashes their poor
true facades.

Rodríguez's stylistic kinship with baroque poetry is not surprising, for he shares its vision of language as a deceptive mask,
and of the duplicity of words as a reflection of the duplicity of
other signs. The next verse-paragraph develops a series of paradoxical antitheses:

La nieve, tan querida
otro tiempo, nos ciega,
no da luz. Copo a copo,
como ladrón, recela
al caer . . .
Tan sin dolor, su entrega
es crueldad. Cae, cae,
hostil al canto, lenta,
bien domada, bien dócil,
como sujeta a riendas
que nunca se aventuran
a conquistar. No riega
sino sofoca, ahoga
dando no amor, paciencia.

                                        (159–60)

The snow, so beloved
in another time, blinds us,
gives no light. Flake by flake,
like a thief, it is suspicious
as it falls.
With so little pain, its surrender
is cruelty. It falls, it falls,

hostile to song, slow,
well-tamed, docile,
as if subjected to reins
that never venture
to conquer. It does not irrigate
but suffocates, drowns,
giving not love, patience.

The first opposition, blindness versus light, is a conventional
one, although the whiteness of the snow is usually associated
with light rather than with darkness. The other antitheses in this
passage exploit the contradictory connotations of words. The
word *dolor* (in its positive sense) is opposed to *entrega* (normally
positive in Rodríguez's poetry) and to *crueldad; amor* stands
opposed to *paciencia; hostil* is equated with *domada* and *dócil.*
This language is consistent in its condemnation of cowardice,
complacency, and passivity. Still, the paradoxes have the effect
of revealing the ambiguity and arbitrariness of the sign, under-
mining the correspondence between signifier and signified.

The subversion of the sign, of course, also occurs on the
thematic level. The poem concludes with yet another appeal to
the unmasking of deceptive appearances:

Y borró los caminos.
Y tú dices: "despierta,
que amanece." (Y es noche
muy noche.) Dices: "cierra,
que entra sol." Y no quiero
perder de nuevo ante esta
nevada. No, no quiero
mentirte otra vez. Tengo
que alzarle la careta
a este rostro enemigo
que me finge a mi puerta
la inocencia que vuelve
y el pie que deja huella.

(160)

And it erased the roads.
And you say: "Wake up,
It's dawn." (And it is night
very night.) You say: "close it,
the sun's coming in." And I do not want
to lose again before this
snowfall. No, I do not want

to lie to you once again. I must
raise the mask
of this enemy face
that fakes at my door
the returning innocence
and the foot that leaves its print.

The speaker's companion, half-asleep, is deceived by the brightness of the snow, which produces a false dawn. This other voice
could either be a lover or an alter ego; in either case it represents
his own impulse to give in to deception. This time the speaker
resolves to lift the mask and face the truth with no illusion. The
deceptiveness of the snow is particularly insidious because it is
double: it not only conceals the ugly reality underneath it, but it
pretends to do so without guile. It seems to offer a return to
innocence and thus the possibility of a new beginning. Having
covered up the roads, it invites the creation of new paths. The
final line of the poem leaps from the image of the snow to that of
the footprint. In semiotic terms this print is an *indexical* sign,
one that signifies through an actual connection with its object.
The snow, then, falsely suggests that the poet can leave a direct
trace of his footsteps, thus creating a new version of his self, freed
of the guilt and deception of the past.

In "Cáscaras" and "Nieve en la noche" the poet sees the signifier as a mask for the signified: the word contains its meaning
even as it conceals it. This image of the sign is a frequent one in
the hermeneutical tradition. Interpretation is the process of unmasking the literal meaning in order to arrive at the truth contained within the text, the content within the form. Rodríguez's
use of these *topoi*, however, often subverts this tradition, for the
"truth" to be found behind language is a purely negative one. The
poet discovers behind the facade the tautological truth that this
facade is deceptive: the arbitrariness of the sign allows him a
vision of the arbitrariness of the sign.

The attempt to unmask language, then, does not necessarily
imply that there is anything of value behind it: "muerde aunque
nunca llegues," the poet commands—search for the truth even
though there is no certainty that you will ever find it. Furthermore, the process of unmasking the sign is not as simple as it
might appear. The distinction between signifier and signified, the
husk and the kernel of meaning it contains, is not always so
straightforward. "Gestos," the poem that immediately follows

"Brujas a mediodía," emphasizes the ambiguity of the sign rather than its deceptiveness. It is not that the sign appears to say one thing on the surface while concealing its true meaning (a lack of correspondence between signifier and signified) but that its very surface is slippery and indeterminate.[12]

"Gestos" represents one of Rodríguez's most explicitly semiotic poems: it is one of the two poems in *Alianza* that directly speaks of "significación."[13] It also provides the clearest example of the interrelationship between his meditation on the sign and his social and ethical preoccupations. The poem begins with a veiled political reference. The Spanish people can find salvation through a more authentic relation to the sign:

> Una mirada, un gesto,
> cambiarán nuestra raza. Cuando actúa mi mano,
> tan sin entendimiento y sin gobierno,
> pero con errabunda resonancia,
> y sondea, buscando
> calor y compañía en este espacio
> en donde tantas otras
> han vibrado, ¿qué quiere
> decir?
>
> (131)

> A glance, a gesture,
> will change our race. When my hand acts,
> with so little understanding or government,
> but with wandering resonance,
> and probes, searching
> for warmth and company in this space
> in which so many others
> have vibrated, what
> does it mean?

The tone becomes more doubtful after the first sentence. The groping movement of the speaker's hand is at once a search for understanding and for social solidarity, for truth and for love. Read in isolation, this passage might not appear metapoetic. In the context of Rodríguez's theory of the poetic act as an epistemological exploration of reality, however, the poet's gestures become a metaphor for the process of creation. The poet begins writing without knowing what the final result will be, and allows language itself to suggest the direction in which he will proceed. "La poesía," Rodríguez has suggested, "es una aventura lingüística" [Poetry is a linguistic adventure].[14]

The poet's gesture is not only a search for meaning but also a sign to be interpreted. The most fundamental characteristic of this sign is its arbitrary randomness:

> Cuántos y cuántos gestos como
> un sueño mañanero
> pasaron. Como esa
> casera mueca de las figurillas
> de la baraja, aunque
> dejando herida o beso, sólo azar entrañable.

> How many, how many gestures like
> a morning dream
> passed by. Like that
> homemade grimace of the little figures
> of the deck of cards, although
> leaving a wound or a kiss, only intimate chance.

The metaphor of the chance configuration of a deck of cards points to a potential risk in the poet's irrational, intuitive approach to the sign. His linguistic play, which aims both to reveal some truth and to bring him into contact with other human beings, might produce only haphazard and therefore meaningless permutations of language. Both its negative and its positive meanings ("herida o beso") are basically accidental and contingent.

The random character of the sign, then, produces an ethical ambiguity as well as a semiotic one:

> Más luminoso aún que la palabra,
> nuestro ademán, como ella
> roído por el tiempo, viejo como la orilla
> del río, ¿qué
> significa?
> ¿Por qué desplaza el mismo aire el gesto
> de la entrega o del robo,
> el que cierra una puerta o el que la abre,
> el que da luz o apaga?
> ¿Por qué es el mismo el giro del brazo cuando siembra
> que cuando siega,
> el del amor que el del asesinato?

> More luminous even than the word,
> our gesture, like the word
> gnawed by time, old as the riverbank,
> what does it signify?

Why do they displace the same air, the gesture
of giving up and robbing,
that which closes the door and that which opens,
that which gives light and that which extinguishes it?
Why is the arc of the arm the same when it sows
as when it reaps,
that of love and that of murder?

The gesture is more "luminous" than the word because it is a
motivated sign, one that directly reveals its meaning. Such "body
language," in contrast to duplicitous speech, does not even seem
to call for interpretation: "actions speak louder than words." This
transparence is nevertheless illusory, for the meaning, indeed the
very identity of the gestural sign, is duplicitous. Two diametrically opposed "speech-acts"—giving and robbing, opening
and closing, and so on—share an identical signifier. The gesture
is at the same time more motivated and more ambiguous than the
word, more closely connected to its meaning and more indeterminate.

The paradoxical status of the gesture dramatizes the speaker's
ambivalence toward all signs. The second verse-paragraph re-
prises the political theme with which the poem began:

> Nosotros, tan gesteros pero tan poco alegres,
> raza que sólo supo
> tejer banderas, raza de desfiles,
> de fantasías y de dinastías,
> hagamos otras señas.
> No he de leer en cada palma, en cada
> movimiento, como antes. No puedo ahora frenar
> la rotación inmensa del abrazo
> para medir su órbita
> y recorrer su emocionada curva.
> No, no son tiempos
> de mirar con nostalgia
> esa estela infinita del paso de los hombres.
>
> (131–32)

> We, so gesticulating but so little happy,
> race that only knew
> how to sew flags, race of parades,
> of fantasies and dynasties,
> let us make other signs.
> I must not read in every palm, in each
> movement, like before. I cannot now restrain

> the immense rotation of the embrace
> to measure its orbit,
> and rerun its emotional curve.
> No, these are not times
> to regard nostalgically
> that infinite wake of men's footsteps.

The poet's call for "other signs" to replace the empty and duplicitous gestures of political propaganda, which the poet must
view with suspicion, clearly establishes the connection between
his social and his linguistic denunciation. A cultural stereotype
(Spaniards speak with their hands) serves to reveal a deeper
characteristic of the "race": the propensity to substitute illusion
for reality. The contrast between an illusory glory in the past, a
decadence in the present, and a hope for the future recalls
Campos de Castilla. Like Machado, the speaker here rejects
nostalgia. Instead, he looks forward to the creation of a new
language, one that he will no longer be obliged to distrust:

> Hay mucho que olvidar
> y más aún que esperar. Tan silencioso
> como el vuelo del búho, un gesto claro,
> de sencillo bautizo,
> dirá, en un aire nuevo,
> mi nueva significación, su nuevo
> uso. Yo sólo, si es posible,
> pido, cuando me llegue la hora mala,
> la hora de echar de menos tantos gestos queridos,
> tener fuerza, encontrarlos
> como quien halla un fósil
> (acaso una quijada aún con el beso trémulo)
> de una raza extinguida.

$$(132)$$

> There is much to forget
> and still more to hope. As silent
> as the owl's flight, a clear gesture,
> of simple baptism,
> will say, in a new air,
> my new signification, its new
> use. I only ask,
> if it is possible, that when the evil hour comes,
> the hour of missing so many beloved gestures,
> to have strength, to find them
> as one finds a fossil

(perhaps a jaw with the kiss still trembling)
of an extinguished race.

Several critics have emphasized Rodríguez's irrationalism, which they find to be reminiscent of the Surrealist movement.[15] In this case, however, the poet evokes the owl, a traditional symbol of reason and wisdom. The analogy of baptism implies at once a ritual cleansing of guilt, a rebirth, and an inaugural act of naming. The new sign will be transparent: "claro" and "sencillo" rather than opaque and arbitrary. The poet imagines himself in the future as a sort of paleontologist of his own people, able to recover the fossil of this authentic language.

"Gestos," in its movement from a skeptical vision of social language toward a renovation of the sign, is a microcosm of *Alianza y condena*. Although the poem serves to illustrate the poet's consciousness of the arbitrariness of all human communication, it also reveals the link between this arbitrariness and the renewal of hope. Paradoxically, it is only through his recognition of the ambiguity of the sign that the poet is able to transcend his narrowly critical view of the world.

The vision of the sign in a poem such as "Nieve en la noche" is doubly negative: language is essentially deceptive, and it con-ooalo an unploaoant roality but rathor a neutral signifier that can much more radical. The movement of the arm is not so much deceptive as it is arbitrary: it is not a pleasant facade that conceals an unplasant reality but rather a neutral signifier that can refer to either violence or love. This radical arbitrariness allows the poet to go beyond the purely critical vision, as in the conclusion of "Gestos." The poems considered thus far are included in the first and second of the four sections or "libros" of *Alianza y condena*. The poems in "Libro tercero" invert the critical vision of language. Just as a seemingly negative sign can conceal a negative truth, the reverse is also possible: this negative "truth" can be the deceptive sign for another, more positive reality.

Rodríguez tends to be a resolutely anticonfessional writer. The poems of the third section of *Alianza*, however, are among his most intensely personal. As their titles reveal, several appear to refer to specific events: "Un suceso" (An event), "Hacia un recuerdo" (Toward a memory), "Un momento" (A moment). The indefinite article—"Un olor," "Una luz," "Un bien"—indicates the particularity of these experiences. At the same time, the anecdote is rarely explicit: an unnamed act of betrayal, which produces guilt and remorse, underlies several poems. As in *Conjuros*, the poet-protagonist attempts to atone for this unspecified failing in his past.

As Mudrovic observes, many of the poems in this section are based on the same paradox: "from evil, good arises."[16] The poet attempts to find redeeming value in his negative experience: "Ya se sabe / que el escorpión, la sanguijuela, el piojo / curan a veces" (182) [It is well known / that the scorpion, the leech, the flea / cure at times]. The critic does not, however, consider this paradox in terms of Rodríguez's preoccupation with the sign. In "Un bien," good is concealed behind a deceptive veil; the poem employs the image of clothing, a traditional metaphor for the signifier: "A veces, mal vestido un bien nos viene; / casi sin ropa, sin acento, como / de una raza bastarda" (184) [At times, badly dressed something good comes to us; / almost without clothes, without accent, as if / of a bastard race]. The poet's task, then, is to recognize the good in its shabby dress, to interpret a seemingly insignificant or negative sign in more transcendent terms.[17] (This deciphering of the sign is a symmetrical reversal of the critical vision, the attempt to unmask the wolf in sheep's clothing.) The metaphor of song relates the interpretive activity to poetry itself: "¿Estamos sordos / a su canción tan susurrada, pobre / de notas?" [Are we deaf / to its song, so whispered, poor / in notes?].

"Como el son de las hojas del álamo" (Like the sound of the poplar leaves), like other poems in the third book, is based on the paradox of the negative sign. In this case, however, it is not a simple matter of "un bien" "mal vestido": the poem actually demonstrates the process by which a negative sign is transformed into an ambiguous and therefore potentially positive one. Along with "Gestos" and "Cáscaras," it is one of Rodríguez's most explicitly metalingual poems. The poem begins with the transformation of an emotion into a sound:

> El dolor verdadero no hace ruido;
> deja un susurro como el de las hojas
> del álamo mecidas por el viento,
> un rumor entrañable, de tan honda
> vibración, tan sensible al menor roce,
> que puede hacerse soledad, discordia,
> injusticia o despecho.

(178)

> True sorrow makes no noise;
> it leaves a whisper like that of the leaves

of the poplar swayed by the wind,
an intimate rumor, so sensitive to the least touch,
that it can become solitude, discord,
injustice or spite.

After converting his "dolor" into an auditory sound, the poet proceeds to interpret this sign. Like the branches of a tree, the sound bifurcates, becoming a "susurro," a "rumor," and a "vibración." This multiplication of the signifier also yields new signifieds: a rather abstract emotion, "dolor," which can denote either physical pain or mental suffering, takes on a series of more concrete meanings. This process continues in the following lines:

> Estoy oyendo
> su murmurado son, que no alborota
> sino que da armonía, tan buido
> y sutil, tan timbrado de espaciosa
> serenidad, que casi es ya cordura dolorosa,
> pura resignación.

> I am hearing
> its murmured sound, which does not disturb
> but gives harmony, so polished
> and subtle, so tempered with spacious
> serenity, that now it is almost painful tenderness,
> pure resignation.

There are a few significant changes here: the sound begins to gain independence from the emotion it originally represented. At the same time its original referent, the "dolor" of the first line, loses some of its negative connotations. Instead of "injusticia o despecho," the speaker experiences more ambivalent and even positive feelings: serenity, sanity, and resignation. The adjective "pura" is significant here, for the original emotion is undergoing a process of purification. It is being neutralized through its transformation into music, an automous system of signs.

The next lines refer to the source of the poet's sorrow, an unidentified act of betrayal in the past:

> Traición que vino
> de un ruin consejo de la seca boca
> de la envidia. Es lo mismo. Estoy oyendo
> lo que me obliga y enriquece, a costa
> de heridas que aún supuran.

> Betrayal that came
> from the despicable advice of envy's
> dry mouth. It is the same. I am hearing
> that which obliges and enriches me, at the cost
> of wounds that are still oozing.

It is unclear whether the speaker was the perpetrator or the victim of this betrayal. Perhaps it does not matter ("Es lo mismo"), for by purifying the emotion he abolishes all distinctions, converting the event into a polyvalent sign with both negative and positive meanings. The conclusion of the poem makes explicit the semiotic nature of the sound:

> Dolor que oigo
> muy recogidamente, como a fronda
> mecida, sin buscar señas, palabras
> o significación. Música sola,
> sin enigmas, son solo que traspasa
> mi corazón, dolor que es mi victoria.

> Sorrow that I hear
> very quietly, like a swaying
> frond, without seeking signs, words,
> or signification. Music alone,
> without enigmas, sound alone that pierces
> my heart, sorrow that is my victory.

At this point the purification of the poet's sorrow is complete. The sound, originally a sign for this emotion, has become an autonomous signifier, a purely musical sign that no longer calls for interpretation. The poet has triumphed over his emotion by transforming it into a sign, exploring this sign's ambiguity, and finally asserting its autonomy. The poem moves from "dolor" to "resignación," and, in the paradox of the last line, to "victoria."

"Como el son de las hojas del álamo," like "Brujas a mediodía" and "Gestos," exemplifies a basic paradigm at work in Alianza y condena as a whole. In each of these poems the poet's starting point is a predominately negative view of both language and reality. Through a meditation on the arbitrariness of the sign he is able to rediscover a more hopeful vision. Perhaps the best way of understanding this process is through an examination of the title of the collection. The most obvious reading is a direct contrast between the two terms: "alliance" versus "condemnation."[18] As José Luis Cano has exclaimed: "alianza con ese sol que brilla puro, con esa patria desnuda y verdadera . . . condena de todo lo que ensucia, con su falsedad, su impureza, la verdad de una tierra y de un pueblo" [alliance with that sun that shines purely, with that true and naked fatherland . . . condemnation of everything that dirties, with its falseness, its impurity, the truth of a land and its people].[19] *Alianza*, however, can also be a negative concept. The word can refer to an alliance in the military sense, a social contract built on fear rather than love. In this second interpretation, "alliance as condemnation," a fearful defensiveness stands in contrast to true social communion: "¿cómo fortificar aquí la vida / si ella es sólo alianza?" (164) [How can we fortify our life here / if it is only alliance?]. The reading suggested by the poems in the third section, finally, is "alliance in condemnation," or "condemnation as alliance" ("dolor que es mi victoria"). The poet finds paradoxical comfort in his condemnation; he is able to perceive a saving grace in his seemingly miserable circumstances.

As with the paradoxes of "Nieve en la noche," the alternate readings of the title phrase arise from an awareness of the reversibility of terms, the essential ambiguity of words. In the case of the last reading this ambiguity allows for a potential escape from the devastatingly critical vision of language and reality. In "Nieve en la noche" the arbitrariness of the sign allows the poet to strip away the pleasant illusions of reality in order to face the negative truth. The same principle of arbitrariness, however, ultimately leads him to question this "truth" as yet another deceptive sign. His consciousness of the duplicity of language can be liberating as well as destructive.

The sign in *Alianza y condena* is essentially ambiguous; it is potentially either true or deceitful, positive or negative. Thus the critical vision that dominates many of the poems of the first two sections can be reversed: the poet's salvation appears to him disguised in a destructive form. The unmasking of a positive reality concealed by an apparently negative sign leads to a final possibility, a language that truly coincides with its positive referent. The two somewhat longer-than-average poems that comprise the fourth and final section of the book, "Oda a la niñez" (Ode to childhood) and "Oda a la hospitalidad" (Ode to hospitality), explore the possibility of a return to a more innocent vision of the sign. The desire for a simpler relation to the world expressed in these poems recalls the pastoral aspirations of *Don de la ebriedad* and *Conjuros*. In these final poems of Rodríguez's third volume, however, the poet retains his awareness of the dangers of self-deception. Ever conscious of the duplicity of language, he searches for a paradoxical "wise innocence" that will overcome the powerful sense of disillusionment that dominates the earlier poems in the book.

Like many other poems in *Alianza*, "Oda a la niñez" begins on a negative note. The return of innocence takes the ironical form of a cold March day:

> ¿Y esta es tu bienvenida,
> marzo, para salir de casa alegres:
> con viento húmedo y frío de meseta?
> Siempre ahora, en la puerta,
> y aún a pesar nuestro, vuelve, vuelve
> este destino de niñez que estalla
> en todas partes: en la calle, en esta
> voraz respiración del día, en la
> sencillez del primer humo sabroso,
> en la mirada, en cada laboreo
> del hombre.
>
> (187)

> Is this your welcome,
> March, so that we are happy to leave our houses,
> with the cold damp wind from the plain?
> Always at this moment, at the door,
> and even in spite of ourselves, it returns,
> this destiny of childhood that bursts
> everywhere returns: in the street, in this
> voracious respiration of the day, in the
> simplicity of the first savory bone,
> in looking, in each work
> of man.

This "destino de niñez" is presented as an exception to the normal world of everyday life in the city, with its overarching sense of defeat and its "confuso vocerío" [confused yelling]:

> Entonces,
> nada hay que nos aleje
> de nuestro hondo oficio de inocencia.
>
> (187–88)

> Then
> there is nothing that takes us away
> from our deep office of innocence.

This last phrase, which echoes the earlier "destino de niñez," provides an essential key to the poet's attitude. Innocence here is not a natural state that can simply be taken for granted, but rather an "oficio," a craft or trade and a calling as well (the word has strong ecclesiastical connotations). Moreover, the return to innocence is frightening: it is presented as a "castigo" [punishment] and a "combate" [combat].

The alternation between the negative circumstances of everyday life and the return of hope continues throughout "Oda a la niñez." The second of the four roman-numeraled sections consists of a litany of denunciations, reminiscent of many earlier poems of *Alianza*. This section culminates in a rhetorical question—"¿Por qué todo es infancia?" (189) [Why is everything childhood?]—that leads to the refrain in the third section, "Ved que todo es infancia" (189–90) [Behold that everything is childhood]. This phrase introduces a new list of circumstances, mostly negative, in the poet's everyday life, including a condemnation of the bankruptcy of language:

> Ved que todo es infancia.
> . . . .
> nuestras
> palabras que ahora,
> al saludar, quisieran
> ser pañales y son
> telas de araña, nuestra
> violencia hereditaria,
> la droga del recuerdo, la alta estafa del tiempo,
> la dignidad del hombre
> que hay que abrazar y hay
> que ofrecer y hay
> que salvar aquí mismo,
> en medio de esta lluvia fría de marzo . . .
> Ved que todo es infancia.
>
> (189–90)

> Behold that everything is childhood.
> . . . .
> our
> words that now,
> as we greet, would like
> to be honeycombs and are
> spiderwebs, our
> hereditary violence,
> the drug of memory, the high fraud of time

> the dignity of man
> that we must embrace and
> offer and
> save right here,
> in the middle of the cold March wind . . .
> Behold that everything is childhood.

The appearance of a more positive element such as "la dignidad del hombre" in this list is surprising. Even more strange is the grouping together of these diverse elements under the general heading of "infancia." (None of the conventional associations of childhood enters into the picture.) It is as if the poet were attempting to reduce his experience in all of its complexity into a single word, one that connotes innocence, purity, and happiness—everything that this experience is not.

The fourth and final section of "Oda a la niñez" further defines the poet's paradoxical conception of childhood:

> Lo de entonces fue sueño. Fue una edad. Lo de ahora
> no es presente o pasado,
> ni siquiera futuro: es el origen.
>
> (190)

> Then it was a dream. It was an age. Now
> it is not present or past,
> nor even future: it is the origin.

It is clear that the poet does not desire a nostalgic return to a happier time: as always, he rejects nostalgia.[20] Rather, he wishes to regain a sense of the pristine innocence of the world, an almost mystical state that can occur even in the worst of circumstances:

> Y nadie,
> nada hay que nos aleje
> de nuestro oficio de felicidad
> sin distancia ni tiempo.
> Es el momento ahora
> en el que, quién lo diría, alto, ciego, renace
> el sol primaveral de la inocencia,
> ya sin ocaso sobre nuestra tierra.
>
> (190–91)

> And there is no one,
> nothing that takes us away
> from our deep office of happiness

without distance or time.
It is the moment now
in which, who would say it, high, blind,
the spring sun of innocence is reborn
now without sunset over our land.

The "oficio de felicidad" echoes the "oficio de inocencia" of the first section of the poem. The idea of a divine force that re-creates the poet and his fellow human beings calls to mind some similar language in *Don de la ebriedad:* "¿Quién hace menos creados / cada vez a los seres" (1ºI, 33) [Who makes the beings / less and less created]; "El primer surco de hoy será mi cuerpo" (2º "Canto del despertar" 45) [The first furrow today will be my body]. The final line of "Oda a la niñez" contains the central image of Rodríguez's first book, the eternal dawn. As in the visionary poetics of *Don de la ebriedad,* time stops, and the poet witnesses a moment of original creation.

Whereas "Oda a la niñez" is metaphorical journey in time, the final poem of *Alianza y condena,* "Oda a la hospitalidad," is a poem of homecoming. It is significant that Rodríguez, who had been living and teaching in England since 1957, returned to live in Spain in 1965, the year of *Alianza's* publication. "Oda a la hospitalidad" begins with the image of a wanderer in search of comfort:

> En cualquier tiempo y en cualquier terreno
> siempre hay un hombre que
> anda tan vagabundo como el humo,
> bienhechor, malhechor,
> bautizado con la agria
> leche de nuestras leyes. Y él encuentra
> su salvación en
> la hospitalidad.
>
> (192)

> In every time and in every terrain
> there is always a man who
> walks, as vagabond as smoke,
> do-gooder, evildoer,
> baptized with the sour
> milk of our laws. And he finds
> his salvation in
> hospitality.

The pattern found in "Oda a la niñez" is evident here as well: the wanderer, clearly the poet's double, finds salvation in spite of his circumstances:

> Forastero, ve cómo
> una vieja mentira se hace una verdad nueva.
> Ve el cuerpo del engaño
> y lo usa: esa puerta
> que, al abrirse, rechina
> con cruel desconfianza, con amargo reproche . . .

> A stranger, he sees how
> an old lie becomes a new truth.
> He sees the body of deceit
> and uses it: that door
> that, upon opening, squeaks
> with cruel distrust, with bitter reproach . . .

Returning to his native land as a stranger, the protagonist must virtually reinvest his past:

> ¿Mas alguien puede
> hacer de su pasado
> simple materia de revestimiento:
> cera, laca, barniz, lo que muy pronto
> se marchita, tan pronto,
> como la flor del labio?
> ¿O bien ha de esperar a estar con esos
> verdaderos amigos, los que darán sentido
> a su vida, a su tierra y a su casa?
>
> (193)

> But can anyone
> make of his past
> a simple matter of re-dressing:
> wax, lacquer, varnish, that which very soon
> wilts, as soon
> as the lip's flower?

This revision of the past cannot be a superficial one: after his destruction of illusions in poems such as "Brujas a mediodía" and "Nieve en la noche," the poet rejects the possibility of merely creating another superficial facade.

The final section of the poem contains many echoes of its companion piece. Like "infancia," the key concept of "Oda a la hospitalidad" is associated with a moment of origin:

Es la hospitalidad. Es el origen
de la fiesta y del canto.
Porque el canto es tan sólo
palabra hospitalaria: la que salva
aunque deje la herida.

(194)

It is hospitality. It is the origin
of festival and song.
Because song is only
a hospitable word: that which saves
although it leaves a wound.

Here the moment of innocence is directly tied to a vision of
language in general and of poetry in particular:

A pesar de que hagamos
de convivencia técnicas
de opresión y medidas
de seguridad, y
de la hospitalidad hospicios, siempre
hay un hombre sencillo y una mañana clara,
con la alta transparencia de esta tierra,
y una casa, y una hora
próspera.

Even though we make
living together techniques
of oppression and security
measures, and
hospices of hospitality, there is always
a simple man and a clear morning,
with the high transparence of this earth,
and a house, and a prosperous
hour.

As elsewhere in *Alianza y condena*, simplicity, clarity, and transparency (words associated with the motivation of the sign) stand
in opposition to the deceitful language of a corrupt society. The
link between an inauthentic social order and words that do not
correspond to reality is evident in the play on words: "hospitalidad hospicios."

The concluding lines of "Oda a la hospitalidad" depict a moment of true communal solidarity, rare in Rodríguez's poetry after
Conjuros. Through his act of naming, the poet-wanderer regains
his link to his native land:

Ahora su patria es esta generosa
ocasión y, sereno,
algo medroso ante tal bien, acoge
y nombra, uno por uno,
a sus amigos sin linaje, de
nacimiento. Ya nunca
forastero, en familia,
no con docilidad, con aventura,
da las gracias muy a solas,
como mendigo. Y sabe,
comprende al fin. Y mira alegremente,
con esa intimidad de la llaneza
que es la única eficacia,
los rostros y las cosas,
la verdad de su vida
recién ganada aquí, entre las paredes
de una juventud libre y un hogar sin fronteras.

                                                (194–95)

Now his homeland is this generous
occasion, and, calmly,
somewhat fearful before such a good thing, welcomes
and names, one by one,
his friends without lineage,
from birth. Now never again
a stranger, among family,
not with docility, with adventure,
he gives thanks, very much alone,
like a beggar. And he knows,
he understands in the end. And he looks happily,
with that intimacy of plainness
that is the only efficacy,
at faces and things,
the truth of his life
newly gained here, between the walls
of a free youth and a home without frontiers.

The similarities between these lines and the conclusion of "Oda a la niñez" are evident. In both cases the poet gives thanks for his rediscovery of a vision that dissolves both time and space. "Hospitalidad," like "niñez," represents an exceptional moment of vision when the poet is able to regain a more innocent relationship to the world. The two poems share a "happy ending": the poet concludes both with a sweeping affirmation of faith, one that collapses his complex vision of reality into a single dimension. Were it not for the larger context of *Alianza y condena*, these statements would appear naive. Read within this context, the conclusions of the two poems represent the poet's affirmation of a possibility for a truthful language in spite of the essentially duplicitous nature of the sign.

From one point of view, then, the two odes that conclude *Alianza y condena* represent a rediscovery of the innocence lost in the poet's debunking of illusions. Read in this way, the book as a whole would be the story of the transformation of a negative vision of the sign into a renewed faith in the powers of language to integrate the poet into the world. At the same time, the poet never loses his awareness of the arbitrariness of language in these final poems. In contrast to the "naive" viewpoint expressed in many of the poems in *Conjuros*, he continues to consider reality in all of its complexity. His language remains aware of itself: the achievement of the mystical moment of transcendence is the result of an "oficio," a self-conscious effort to transform a vision of reality through language. An alternate way of viewing the development of the book, then, is as a progression from a critical vision, a relatively simple view of the deceptiveness of signs, toward a more complete view of language. The awareness of language revealed in these poems is no less complex than the critical vision in the beginning. If anything, the poet has transcended the simplistic view that equates the arbitrariness of the sign with the meaninglessness of the world.

Rodríguez's poetry, from his earliest poems through his most recent works, is characterized by its use of paradoxical language. The standard account of the evolution of Rodríguez's poetry posits that the supposedly innocent, exalted, and unreflexive exclamations of *Don de la ebriedad* and *Conjuros* give way to the more meditative tone of his "mature" phase. The poet himself has summarized this development: "A lo mejor esta ebriedad un poco cósmica, sin ideas ni presupuestos morales, se vaya haciendo cada vez más moral, más meditativa" [Probably this drunkenness, which is a little cosmic, without ideas or moral precepts, becomes more and more moral, more meditative].[21] This comparison slights the complexity of the earlier work. Still, there is significant validity to the observation that Rodríguez's later poetry is much more cautious in its affirmation of hope. The powerfully critical vision that characterizes so many of the poems in *Alianza y condena* can never be overcome entirely, even in the most exceptional moments of renewed innocence. *Alianza y condena*, then, ends on a paradoxical note. The trajectory of the volume moves from a distrust of all language toward an innocent view of the sign. Yet this new vision remains aware of its own status as language. It is the principle of the arbitrariness of all signs, in fact, that allows the poet to regain his faith in the word.

In *Alianza y condena*, in short, the tension between opposing visions of the sign and between the opposing visions of reality they imply becomes more acute, while the use of language becomes even more self-conscious. It is this paradoxical vision of language (and language of vision) that Claudio Rodríguez will explore in the poems of *El vuelo de la celebración*.

5

The Language of Paradox and the Paradox of Language: The Later Poetry

A distinctive characteristic of Rodríguez's later work emerges in the poems of *Alianza y condena*: the attempt to fuse the two opposing attitudes toward language. This is not simply a shift away from the belief in the union of language and the world, for the poet never renounces this ideal. At the same time he becomes increasingly aware of the arbitrariness of the link between words and things, and of the impossibility of choosing between this awareness and his commitment to a poetry that attempts to overcome it. This tendency toward the simultaneous consideration of the two opposing facets of the sign culminates in the poems of *El vuelo de la celebración* (The flight of celebration). In this work, and in subsequent poems not yet collected in book-form, the poet remains constantly aware of the contradictions between his opposing aims, the two ideas of language that can be neither separated nor reconciled.[1] The difficult, paradoxical language that characterizes all of Rodríguez's work becomes even more prominent in this later poetry, which focuses more intensely on the fundamental paradox of poetic language.

The contradictory nature of Rodríguez's later work hinders any attempt to form a definitive conclusion about a particular poem. The interpretation of an entire collection of poetry raises even more difficulties. Because of the simultaneous vision of opposing impulses, there is no longer a clearly defined evolution in the poet's consciousness, one that can be traced in a logical way through the course of the volume. This is not to say that *El vuelo de la celebración* cannot be read as a unified work, as an integrated collection of poems. Many interpretations of the collection as a whole are in fact possible. The choice of one reading over another, however, would be somewhat arbitrary. Even the basic question of the fundamental tone of the book is open to debate. Critical commentary on *El vuelo de la celebración* is

113

divided between those who stress its celebratory impulse and those who see it as a more doubtful exploration of reality.

My emphasis, then, will be on the individual poem rather than on the larger structure of the volume. The individual poem, however, is a manifestation of a larger structure: that of Rodríguez's poetic thought as a whole. Each poem is but one version of a single paradigm. Rodríguez's work, always a cohesive system, now turns back on itself. Increasingly, the poet appears to be writing versions of the same poem, refining and distilling the poetic system that he has developed over the course of his career. Explicit allusions to previous texts abound in these poems. Even more significantly, a limited number of symbols, images, and words recur again and again. This "intratextual" technique calls to mind the densely woven semantic web of Vicente Aleixandre's later poetry, which Pere Gimferrer has defined as "an *ars combinatoria* that proceeds by permutation, substitution, or superposition of an extremely limited repertory of elements. . . . What is truly surprising and worthy of admiration . . . is the fact that said elements have such a polysemic value that their reappearance goes unnoticed by the common reader and is only perceptible to the analyst."[2] This distinction, however, is debatable, for it is impossible to predict what a hypothetical "common reader" of poetry will or will not notice. How long can one read such difficult poetry without beginning to analyze it? It could be argued that the attempt to make sense of a larger paradigm is an integral part of the reading experience in both Rodríguez's and Aleixandre's work. The paradigmatic dimension of *El vuelo de la celebración* makes any diachronic interpretation of the work—as a trajectory from point A to point B—very arbitrary. Readers who undertake a difficult book of poetry such as this would not normally begin with the first poem and proceed, in order, to the last, as they would read a novel. They would jump from poem to poem, comparing, contrasting, and making connections. Their ultimate understanding of the work would depend more on these paradigmatic relations than on the particular order in which the poems are arranged.

In *El vuelo de la celebración*, as in all of Rodríguez's work, the relation of signifier to signified implies a relation between the poet and reality. This equivalence between the structure of the sign and the poet's place in the world is fundamental to Rodríguez's poetics at all stages of his career, for it means that poetic language itself will determine the degree of the poet's integration. The motivation of the sign always carries with it the ideal of participation, or loss of distance, while the arbitrariness of the sign directly correlates with alienation and critical vision. *Don de la ebriedad* sets forth a paradigm in which the poet seeks to gain his salvation by participating in the world. He envisions the gap between signifier and signified, or between language and reality, as an obstacle to a full surrender of his alienated consciousness. In Rodríguez's subsequent two books the relation between participation and critical vision becomes increasingly complicated, for the poet-protagonist is no longer able to renounce his consciousness of the arbitrariness of language, which is also an awareness of his own ultimate estrangement from the world. The motivation of the sign allows the poet to participate in the world, yet this motivation is illusory and thus robs this participation of its authenticity.

There is a tendency among many of Rodríguez's critics to treat the impulse toward participation as primary, and even to ignore the opposing movement away from the world. Rodríguez himself identifies with John Keats's notion of "negative capability," which he sees as the ability to break down the barrier between the self and the world: "El poeta tiende a convertirse, y de aquí la deformación, en el objeto del poema. Si haces un poema sobre una pared, o lo que sea, el proceso creador te lleva a prescindir de tu personalidad; ésa es su capacidad negativa, decía Keats" [The poet tends to convert himself, and here is the deformation, into the object of the poem. If you do a poem about a wall, or whatever it might be, the creative process brings you to do without your personality; this is negative capability, said Keats].[3]

Many of Rodríguez's poems follow a paradigm in which the poet approaches an object with an attitude of contemplation, and subsequently seeks to participate in the object, to lose himself in it. Gonzalo Sobejano has analyzed several of Rodríguez's poems in terms of a three-step process of "advenimiento," "epifanía," and "integración."[4] "Espuma" (Foam), one of the best-known poems of *Alianza y condena*, follows this paradigm. It begins with the "advenimiento," an act of vision:

> Miro la espuma, su delicadeza
> que es tan distinta a la de la ceniza.
> Como quien mira una sonrisa, aquella
> por la que da su vida y le es fatiga
> y amparo, miro ahora la modesta
> espuma.

(151)

I look at the foam, its delicacy
that is so different from that of ash.
As one who looks at a smile, that
for which he gives his life, and it is fatigue
and shelter for him, I look now at the modest
foam.

The next stage is the epiphany, which Sobejano, following Joyce, defines as "súbita manifestación espiritual, dinámico momento de contacto" [sudden spiritual manifestation, dynamic moment of contacto]:[5]

Es el momento bronco y bello
del uso, el roce, el acto de la entrega
creándola. El dolor encarcelado
del mar, se salva en fibra tan ligera.
Bajo la quilla, frente al dique, donde
existe el amor surcado, como en tierra
la flor, nace la espuma. Y es en ella
donde rompe la muerte, en su madeja
donde el mar cobra ser, como en la cima
de su pasión el hombre es hombre, fuera
de otros negocios, en su leche viva.

It is the hoarse and beautiful moment
of use, the friction, the act of surrender
creating it. The imprisoned pain
of the sea is saved in so light a fiber.
Under the prow, against the dike, where
furrowed love exists, as in the earth
the flower, foam is born. And it is in it [in her]
where death breaks, in its tangles
where the sea takes on being, as at the height
of his passion man is man, outside
of other affairs, in his live milk.

Finally, the poet attempts to fuse himself with the object. This is the moment of integration:

A este pretil, brocal de la materia,
que es manantial, no desembocadura,
me asomo ahora, cuando la marea
sube, y allí naufrago, allí me ahogo
muy silenciosamente, con entera
aceptación, ileso, renovado
en las espumas imperecederas.

> Over this railing, well-wall of matter,
> which is source, not outlet,
> I lean over now, when the tide
> rises, and there I am shipwrecked, there I drown
> very silently, with complete
> acceptance, unharmed, renovated
> in the imperishable foam.

Several other critics have joined Sobejano in echoing the celebratory tone of *El vuelo de la celebración.* Nancy Mandlove, for
example, claims that the poet achieves the fusion with the object
that is only attempted in *Don de la ebriedad;* "in *Vuelo de la
celebración* Rodríguez has found a solution to the problem of the
separation of mind and body, the corporeal and the incor-
poreal."[6] At the same time, the poet's achievement of his aim of
losing himself in the world is paradoxical. Since his work is
governed by opposing impulses, his success at one aim might
imply a failure at the other. A complete fusion with the world, in
other words, would involve a sacrifice of critical vision. Alan
Bruflat makes the claim that when the poet affirms his vision
with too little ambivalence, the poem becomes less successful in
involving the reader actively in the creation of meaning. The
poet's fusion with the world, in other words, must seem earned
from the reader's point of view. Otherwise there is the danger of
sentimentality, of achieving a mystical communion that excludes
the reader: "Since the key to Rodríguez's poetic vision is ambivalence—toward earthly reality, poetic reality, and the power of
language—his better poems highlight that ambivalence rather
than obfuscate it through a consolidated vision."[7]

This attempt to erect reader participation into a criterion of
aesthetic value raises several fundamental questions about the
role of the reader. For many contemporary theorists, the reader
necessarily creates the meaning of the text. The text, in other
words, cannot exclude an activity that is inherent in the act of
reading itself. If the opportunity for reader participation is a
feature of certain texts and not of others, then the problem becomes one of predicting how an individual will respond to a
given work. To predict reader response, as Bruflat attempts to do,
is ultimately to prescribe a particular kind of reading and thus,
paradoxically, to limit the reader's freedom.

A related question concerns the very definition of readerly
participation. Bruflat defines it in terms of the reader's identification with the speaker of the poem, brought about by the interplay

of various codes and levels of meaning. There are, however, at least two other identifiable varieties of "participation" among Rodríguez's readers. For a critic such as Sobejano, to participate in the poem is to lose oneself in it, to become caught up in the flow of language and to share the poet's vision completely. (This idea of the reader's involvement in the work is quite close to Rodríguez's notion of the poet's participation in the world.) For such a reader, the poet's most satisfying poems would be those such as "Espuma," which do in fact convey a more consolidated vision of reality. Yet another ideal of reader response would privilege those texts that deny the reader easy access or that deliberately thwart his or her identification with the speaker. The irrational language of *Don de la ebriedad*, Rodríguez's most difficult work, obliges the reader to reenact the poet's own interpretive crisis.[8]

Whatever one's view of the desirability of ambivalence in Rodríguez's poetry, there are few cases in which the speaker actually asserts his vision without reservations. Several poems in *El vuelo de la celebración* do end with what appears to be an unambiguous affirmation: "Te estoy acompañando. / No estás solo." (209) [I am accompanying you. / You are not alone]; "en una hoja el resplandor del cielo." (211) [in one leaf the radiance of the sky]. In their contexts, however, these endings make dramatic sense. In spite of his apparently affirmative tone, the speaker is celebrating a moment of salvation that occurs *in spite of* the fundamentally negative nature of reality. He rarely if ever renounces his critical vision in order to achieve the moment of fusion with the object. The critic's task in these cases is to show how the poet reaches the point of transcendence through a series of linguistic transformations (transformations *of* language and transformations *by means of* language). In the conclusion of "Arena" (Sand), the poem that Bruflat uses to demonstrate the supposed exclusion of the reader, the poet-protagonist does not actually achieve union with the object but rather *asks* to be granted such a union. He employs "prayerful" language, language that, instead of depicting what already exists, attempts to bring about a state of affairs by depicting it, or else to compensate for an unsatisfactory situation. In accordance with this prayerful language the speaker's tone is both tentative and plaintive. He even says "please."

> Vuela tú, vuela,
> pequeña arena mía,

canta en mi cuerpo, en cada poro, entra
en mi vida, por favor, ahora que necesito
tu cadencia, ya muy latiendo en luz,
con el misterio de la melodía
de tu serenidad,
de tu honda ternura.

(208)

Fly, you, fly
my small sand,
sing in my body, in each pore, enter
in my life, please, now that I need
your cadence, already beating very much in light,
with the mystery of the melody
of your serenity,
of your deep tenderness.

The simplicity of this conclusion, then, is illusory. Many readers, swayed by the convincing rhetoric of the final three or four lines, might not observe that the speaker is beseeching the sand to help him, rather than celebrating an event that has already occurred. These readers might come to believe that the poet has actually achieved the integration with nature that he has only requested.

Rodríguez's use of paradoxical techniques means that the most celebratory poems will be tenative, and that poems of doubt will lead to celebration. In "Cantata de miedo," for example, the poet focuses on the positive aspects of fear, even going so far as to ask whether it is "el menos traicionero" [the least treacherous] of his companions (224). In a rough census of the way in which Rodríguez ends his poems, the (apparently) uncomplicated affirmation of "Arena" would be the least frequent type of poetic closure. Several poems end with unanswerable rhetorical questions:

¿Dónde, dónde, la oración del mar
y su blasfemia?

("Amarras," 210)

Where, where, the prayer of the sea
and its blasphemy?

Tú, luz, nunca serena,
¿me vas a dar serenidad ahora?

("Hacia la luz," 35)

You, light, never serene,
are you going to give me serenity now?

Pero, ¿por qué me está mirando el aire
con vileza y sin fe?
                                    ("Hermana mentira," 247)

But, why is the air looking at me
with baseness and without faith?[9]

Another frequent variety of ending is the paradoxical celebration
that is asserted *in spite of* reservations: "Miserable el momento si
no es canto" [Miserable the moment if it is not song] ("Salvación
del peligro," 252). For the later Rodríguez the pain of life is the
normal state of affairs. Virtually every poem in *El vuelo*, beginning with "Herida en cuatro tiempos" (Wound in four times),
appears to stem from a deep sorrow, the most explicitly celebratory poems no less. Any kind of transcendence of this norm is
an exception, a healing of the wound that can only be achieved
through a dialectical manipulation of language.

Several of the most striking characteristics of Rodríguez's poetry reveal his close kinship with the mystical tradition. (This
connection has frequently been acknowledged in passing, as in
Sobejano's use of terms such as "advenimiento" and "epifania.")
Like the mystic poet, Rodríguez attempts to fuse himself with the
absolute, although of course he nowhere identifies this absolute
with God. The poet also uses the mystic oxymoron to express the
paradoxical nature of this fusion. A further link to this tradition
is an ambivalence toward language. It is traditional to charac-
terize the mystic poet's attitude toward the verbal medium as one
of distrust. Jorge Guillén, most notably, has explored the poetics
of San Juan de la Cruz in terms of "insufficient language," the
view that poetic language is a necessarily imperfect reflection of
an ineffable experience.[10] The identification of the mystical experience with the pre- or super-linguistic, however, is open to
question. It is true that the process by which the boundaries of
the self are dissolved into the absolute, whether in mystic poetry
or in Rodríguez's work, involves a destruction of language, which
by definition delimits and circumscribes.[11] Seen from another
perspective, however, language is not the belated and insufficient
rendering of the mystical experience, but a central part of this
experience. Kenneth Burke has put forth the convincing argument that the creation of theological language is the culmination

of the human impulse to develop systems of signs to their fullest potential. Far from being a barrier to transcendence, then, language would be the medium of transcendence *par excellence*.[12] It is the capacity of language to go beyond and negate the limits of the physical world that makes both theology and poetry possible.

The destruction of language, then, is but the first step toward the creation of another language. One of the most distinctive features of this language is its use of paradox. Paradox is often seen as a way of overcoming the limitations inherent in language, of taking language beyond itself. From another point of view, however, it is only language that makes paradox possible in the first place. The mystic's burning night, or Rodríguez's predawn illumination, are purely linguistic creations that do not exist in the natural world.[13]

"Lágrima" (Tear), a short poem from *El vuelo de la celebración*, follows, in approximate form, the three-part paradigm outlined by Gonzalo Sobejano: the arrival, the moment of spiritual illumination, and the final integration with the object. At each step of the way, however, this trajectory toward mystical communion is qualified by the speaker's consciousness of language as a medium:

> Cuando el sollozo llega hasta esta lágrima,
> lágrima nueva que eres vida y caes,
> estás cayendo y nunca caes del todo,
> pero me asciendes hasta mi dolor,
> tú, que eres tan pequeña
> y amiga, y silenciosa,
> de armoniosa amargura.
> Con tu sabor preciso me modelas,
> con tu sal que me llega hasta la boca
> que ya no dice nada porque todo lo has dicho.
>
> Lo has dicho tú, agua abierta,
> y este certero engaño
> de la mirada,
> transfigurada por tu transparencia
> me da confianza y arrepentimiento.
> Estás en mi, con tu agua
> que poco a poco hace feraz el llanto.

                                                            (214)

> When sobbing reaches this tear,
> a new tear [you who] are life and fall,
> are falling and never fall completely,

but lift me up to my pain,
you, who are so small
and friendly, and silent,
of harmonious bitterness.
With your precise [necessary] taste you model me,
with your salt that comes up to my mouth
that no longer says anything because you have said it all.

You have said it, open water,
and this accurate deception
of the gaze,
transfigured by your transparence
gives me confidence and repentance.
You are in me, with your water
which little by little makes my lament fertile.

The teardrop here is itself a sign as well as a purely material object. It is a sign, moreover, in several distinct senses. In the first place it is the silent, nonverbal expression of the poet's emotion. It thus contrasts implicitly with verbal language, the words that the speaker does not pronounce. The tear, then, would appear to be a natural, indexical sign, an almost universal symbol that does not mediate between its referent (the poet's emotion) and our consciousness of this reality. At the same time, the phrase "armoniosa amargura," suggests a comparison to the arbitrary sounds of music. The oxymoron, which is also a synesthesia combining the senses of hearing and taste, points to the complexity of the seemingly transparent expression of the poet's sorrow. As in "Como el son de las hojas del álamo," analyzed in the previous chapter, the musical metaphor leads to a neutralization and ultimately a positive valuation of the poet's emotion. It is significant that the speaker never names the occasion of his sorrow, the ultimate referent of the tear. It would be pointless to search for this referent in the poet's biography, for the poem is not "about," say, the death of a loved one, but rather the transformation of emotion through the linguistic medium.[14]

In the second stanza of the poem the poet views the tear in an even more complex way. If at first it was the direct expression of his emotion, it is now a sign that he must reinterpret, as well as a medium for other signs. As a prism or lens through which the poet sees, it transforms his vision in a very literal sense. The phrase "transfigurada por tu transparencia" is an apparent contradiction, for a transparent medium does not normally change what is seen. Metaphorically, however, the slightly blurry vision produced by the tear represents the "certero engaño" of all language. Like Pedro Salinas's "Seguro azar" [certain chance], this "accurate deception" is a succinct definition of the poetic act, which achieves its end in spite of the fundamentally duplicitous nature of its medium.[15]

The duplicitous nature of language produces contradictory results, "confianza y arrepentimiento." As in *Alianza y condena*, the arbitrariness of the sign is both negative and positive in its value. The poet attempts to achieve transcendence through the transfiguration of a negative arbitrariness into a new fertility based on the possibilities of language. In "Lágrima" this transcendence takes the form of the final stage of the mystic progression, the integration with the object. The tear, having originally been a part of the speaker, becomes reintegrated into its source. It is no longer an arbitrary sign, to be viewed as a semiotic medium, but is now the transcendent sign that allows the speaker to put his sorrow to productive ends.

In light of a poem such as "Lágrima," with its careful development of the paradox of language, it is not accurate to speak of Rodríguez's later poetry in terms of the "free play" of meaning.[16] For all of its complexity and ambivalence, this poetry tends toward a great semantic compression. The same two opposing impulses toward the sign recur in poem after poem. The paradox of "wise innocence," that is, of a fundamental faith in language mitigated, at times even destroyed, by a knowledge of its deceptiveness, is a constant in Rodríguez's poetry from *Alianza y condena* on. In *El vuelo de la celebración* this notion often finds expression in the paradox of an innocent mystery or a mysterious innocence:

> el dolor inocente, que es el mayor misterio
>   ("Herida en cuatro tiempos," 207)

> innocent pain, which is the greatest mystery

> hacia esta luz, tan misteriosa y tan sencilla,
> hacia esta palabra verdadera.
>   ("Hacia la luz," 235)

> toward this light, so mysterious and so simple,
> toward this true word.

> Ahí mismo: en la oscura
> inocencia.

("Ahí mismo," 250)

> Right there: in the dark
> innocence.

Using this method of fragmenting Rodríguez's texts, one could construct a fairly systematic semantic dictionary or concordance of his most characteristic words, phrases, and symbols. In the examples above, mystery and darkness correspond to the opacity of the sign, whereas innocence, simplicity, and light represent the ideal transparence toward which language aspires. By combining these contradictory attributes, Rodríguez is attempting to fuse the two opposing visions of the sign into a single language. The poet approaches the signs of the world with both innocence and suspicion, expecting them to be at once truthful and deceptive. In his desire to integrate himself with the object he surrenders his ego, and at the same time he sees the world as a mystery to be unveiled through the complexity of poetic language.

"Voz sin pérdida" (Voice without loss), one of Rodríguez's most linguistically self-conscious poems, represents his most ambitious attempt so far to fuse the two contradictory impulses toward language. Like many other poems in *El vuelo de la celebración,* it details the poet's contemplation of an object. In this case, significantly, it is the human voice itself that gives rise to his meditation. He considers it as an object, a sign, and, most importantly, the conveyor of other signs. In this way "Voz sin pérdida" resembles poems such as "Gestos" and "Lágrima," which also deal directly with the theme of human communication. In the opening lines, the voice is identified with the March wind, which, as in "Oda a la niñez" and "Viento de primavera" from *Alianza y condena,* is associated with a new beginning:

I.

> Este viento de marzo
> da libertad y bienaventuranza.
> Como tu voz, que es casi luz, almendra
> abierta de misterio y de lujuria,
> con sus tonos astutos, tierna y seca, latiendo
> tan desnuda que limpia la alegría,
> con sus esmaltes y sus ángulos,

sus superficies bien pulimentadas,
no con arrugas, pero
penetrando en mí siempre,
unas veces sumisa y precavida,
trémula de inocencia otras, y en secreto,
bien sé si turbio o si trasparente.

(248)

This March wind
gives freedom and good fortune.
Like your voice, which is almost light, almond
open with mystery and lust,
with its astute tones, tender and dry, beating
so nude that it cleanses happiness,
with its lacquers and its angles,
its well-polished surfaces,
not with wrinkles, but
penetrating in me always,
at times submissive and wary,
tremulous with innocence at other times, and in secret,
well I know whether murky or transparent.

Through this chain of metaphors, many of them found before in
Rodríguez's poems, the speaker emphasizes the materiality of the
voice and thus, by extension, of language. In contrast to the
auditory nature of the voice, tactile images dominate. The sense
of touch normally connotes direct experience rather than the
deciphering of secondary signs. Thus the stress on the pal-
pableness of the voice converts it into an object rather than a
conveyor of information. Toward the end of this passage, however, Rodríguez introduces the binary oppositions with which he
usually considers the double nature of the sign: innocence and
mystery, transparence and confusion, light and darkness. The
metaphors in the following lines alternately emphasize the
earthy materiality of the voice and is transcendent flight toward
the sky:

Su oscuridad, su vuelo
a ras de cielo, como el del vencejo
o a medio aire, como el de la alondra,
su ronquera nocturna, y este viento de marzo
entre tu voz, y la ciudad, y el tráfico . . .

Su terreno rocoso, casi de serranía,
el timbre embravecido y firme, conmovido, escondido

en ese cielo de tu boca, en ese
velo del paladar, tan oloroso como
el laurel, cerca del mar Cantábrico, desde donde
te oigo y amo.

                                                    (248)

Its darkness, its flight
even with the sky, like that of the martin
or in midair, like that of the lark,
its nocturnal hoarseness, in this March wind
among your voice, and the city, and the traffic . . .

Its rocky terrain, almost mountainous,
the timbre, angered and firm, moved, hidden
in that sky of your mouth, in that
veil of the palate, as fragrant as
the laurel, near the Cantabrian Sea, from which
I hear you and love you.

As so often occurs in Rodríguez's poetry, there is a tension in these passages between two metaphorical planes. As the poet develops a series of comparisons involving the bird, the earth, the sky, and the laurel leaves, the reader loses sight of the original object of comparison: the human voice. The effect of this technique, once again, is an emphasis on the materiality of the voice rather than on its communicative function. While the voice takes on other, metaphorical connotations, the signs it conveys are nowhere to be seen. The metonymic expansion in the last few lines, which no longer describe the voice directly but rather connect it with its surroundings, further distracts the reader's attention from the voice as a semiotic medium.

The second section of "Voz sin pérdida" is more explicit in its meditation on language. Whereas the first section moves from the voice toward other metaphors, the conclusion returns to consider the voice explicitly as a sign. The poet's tone becomes more discursive as he details his own reaction to the voice:

II.

He oído y he creído en muchas voces
aunque no en las palabras.
He creído en los labios
mas no en el beso.

                                                    (249)

I have heard and believed in many voices
although not in words.
I have believed in lips
but not in the kiss.

Rodríguez appears to be saying, not that "the medium is the message," but that the medium can be purified of any particular message and thus stand as a sign in its own right. The human voice, although it expresses words, has an autonomy that transcends any message it transmits. Put another way, words detract from the purity of their medium, the voice. The kiss is exactly parallel to the word. Like the act of speech, it is a sign that promises love but ultimately betrays its medium.[17]

The beginning of the following stanza is ambiguous:

En tu voz, más poblada que tu cuerpo,
en el camino hacia
la cadera de tu entonación,
hacia lo que me acoge y me calienta,
hacia tu aliento, tu aire, tu amor puro
entre el pulmón y la laringe: siempre
con la luz dentro, aunque ahora oiga mentiras,
con el amanecer de la palabra
en el cielo mohoso y estrellado de la boca.

(249)

In your voice, more habitated than your body,
in the road toward
the hip of your intonation,
toward that which welcomes me and warms me,
toward your breath, your air, your pure love
between your lungs and your larynx: always
with light inside, although now I hear lies,
with the daybreak of the word
in the mossy and starry sky of your mouth.

The reader does not know whether to understand his companion's voice as something the poet does or does not believe in. One can read either "he creído en los labios . . . en tu voz," or "mas no en el beso . . . [no] en tu voz." The first alternative seems more probable, for the voice, as in the previous verse-paragraph, is the medium for the sign rather than the sign itself. It can thus be purified of meaning and transformed into a new sign: "el amanecer de la palabra." This baroque analogy involves four elements: *boca* is to *palabra* as *cielo* is to [*sol*]. It thus links the theme of language to the single most persistent image in Rodríguez's poetry, the dawn—a moment of new beginning in which the world is no longer deceptive.

In the poet's insistence on the separation of message from medium, words from voice, there is no suggestion that his beloved is a particularly deceitful person. The important point is that any use of language implies deceit because of the duplicitous nature of the sign itself. In the final stanza of "Voz sin pérdida," the words themselves lie, not the person who uses them:

> Que mientan ellas, las palabras tuyas.
> Yo quiero su sonido: ahí, en él, tengo
> la verdad de tu vida, como el viento,
> ya sereno, de marzo. Oyelo. Habla.

(249)

> Let them lie, your words.
> I want their sound: there, in it, I have
> the truth of your life, like the wind,
> now calm, of March. Listen to it. It speaks.

These lines repeat the move toward the purification of language that occurs in "Como el son de las hojas del álamo" and in "Lágrima." Faced with the problem of deceit inherent in all signs, the poet's response is to create an autonomous signifier, severed of its connection with the signified. The last lines of "Voz sin pérdida," however, return to the initial image of the March wind and thus identify the voice with nature. Now there is no longer any gap between signifier and signified: the wind expresses a meaning that is totally identical to its form. The obsession with the materiality of the voice in this poem calls to mind the aspiration toward a "natural language" found in two poems from *Don de la ebriedad:* "Cuándo hablaré de ti sin voz de hombre," and "Como si nunca hubiera sido mía." These poems explicitly call for the merging of the poet's duplicitous human voice with the natural world. In the final lines of "Voz sin pérdida," then, the poet attempts to fuse his two contradictory impulses toward the sign by evoking a speech that is at once autonomous and motivated, transcendent and material. His own poetic language brilliantly plays with the contradictory nature of signs that are both autonomous objects and meaningful words.

El vuelo de la celebración could be said to complete the exploration of the problems of poetic language begun over twenty years before in *Don de la ebriedad*. Rodríguez's first work posed difficult questions concerning the interrelationships between the poet, his language, and the world. Each subsequent work has further developed these problems. *Conjuros* explores the notion of poetic participation first suggested in *Don*, while *Alianza y condena* struggles with the conflict between this participation and the critical distance needed to reach the truth. Although Claudio Rodríguez's work is far from finished, his later poems attempt to synthesize his poetic thought rather than to move it in a fundamentally new direction. As has often been noted, the poet has been writing less and less in recent years. Throughout his career, each new book has taken longer to appear than the previous one. With the increasing use of motifs and topoi from his previous work, Rodríguez is elaborating versions of same poem, the same paradigm of poetic vision.[18]

In his effort to elaborate this paradigm, the later Rodríguez often employs words, images, and even direct quotations from his own previous work. In "Nuevo día" (New day), a poem written after the publication of *El vuelo de la celebración*, virtually every word resonates with intratextual meaning for the reader who is already familiar with Rodríguez's corpus:

> Después de tantos días sin camino,
> y sin dolor siquiera, y las campanas solas,
> y mi cuerpo sin nadie, a la intemperie,
> llega el de hoy.
> Cuando ayer el aliento era misterio
> y la mirada oscura, sin resina,
> buscaba un resplandor definitivo,
> llega tan delicada y tan sencilla,
> tan serena de nueva levadura,
> sin soledad en su fecundación
> sin temor ni peligro, esta mañana
> transparente, con señal tan clara
> de semilla futura, tan entera
> y abierta que casi me obedece y me lo ofrece
> depués del artificio, el hondo engaño
> de la saliva y el estiércol del nido
> y el crisol de un pueblo oscuro.
> Es la aventura de la claridad,
> la inocencia de la contemplación,
> el secreto que se abre con moldura y asombro

esta mañana nunca pasajera,
viva en el alma.
Este momento que no tiene tiempo.[19]

After so many days without road,
and without pain even, and the bells alone,
and my body without anyone, in the elements,
this one of today arrives.
When yesterday my breath was mystery
and my gaze, dark, without resin,
sought a definitive radiance,
it arrives so delicate and so simple,
so serene with new yeast,
without solitude in its fecundation
without fear or danger, this transparent
morning, with so clear a signal
of future seed, so whole
and open that it almost obeys me and offers me
after the artifice, the deep deception
of saliva and the dung of the nest
and the melting-pot of a dark people.
It is the adventure of clarity,
the innocence of contemplation,
the secret that opens with molding and astonishment
this never-fleeting morning,
alive in the soul.
This moment that does not have time.

José Luis García Martín has criticized the obvious repetition of elements from Rodríguez's previous work: "Nada nuevo encontramos en estos poemas: ni el vocabulario, ni la temática, ni los recursos estilísticos (incluso se repite algún sintagma de textos anteriores)" [We find nothing new in these poems: neither vocabulary, nor themes, nor stylistic devices (even some phrases are repeated from previous texts].[20] This observation is accurate as far as it goes, but it overlooks a few important points. In the first place, this poem, perhaps more than any other, distills the paradigm of the language of poetic vision that Rodríguez has been elaborating for more than thirty years. It thus *deliberately* draws upon thematic elements from each of his four previous collections: the visionary poetics of *Don de la ebriedad*, the social concerns of *Conjuros* and *Alianza y condena* ("El crisol de un pueblo oscuro"), and the reversibility of the sign that increasingly characterizes his later work. "Es la aventura de la claridad / la inocencia de la contemplación," is one of

Rodríguez's most succinct definitions of his own poetics, a search for a vision that is both wise and innocent, critical and participatory.

"Nuevo día," furthermore, is self-consciously concerned precisely with the problem of writing a *new poem*. Thus the critic's observation as to the lack of novelty becomes highly ironic. The echoes from previous poems serve to underscore the speaker's anxiety about the renovation of his poetic vision. This anxiety is itself a constant in Rodríguez's work, present already in his first poems. In "Todo es nuevo quizá para nosotros," from *Don de la ebriedad*, as in "Nuevo día," the dawn is at once a truly new event and a repetition of previous dawns.[21] One of the phrases that García Martín probably has in mind, "buscaba un resplandor definitivo," from "Canto del caminar," is also in Rodríguez's first book: "Qué importa la noche si aún estamos / buscando un resplandor definitivo" [What does night matter if we are still / searching for a definitive radiance]. This line, in turn, has its probable source in yet another text, Arthur Rimbaud's *Un saison en l'enfer*: "L'automne déjà!—mais pourquoi regretter un éternel soleil, si nous sommes engagés à la découverte de la clarté divine,—loins des gens qui meurent sur les saisons" [Autumn already—but why regret an eternal sun, if we are engaged in the discovery of divine clarity,—far from the people who die on the season].[22] The point of this exercise is not to uncover Rodríguez's debts nor to debate his novelty but rather to point to the problematic nature of the very concept of "originality," which implies both novelty and a return to the origin.[23] The search for an originary, timeless moment of vision—"Este momento que no tiene tiempo"—is always haunted by these previous unsuccessful attempts at stopping time. The lack of "novelty" in Rodríguez's later work coincides with his awareness of the impossibility of recovering the original moment of poetic illumination.

A poem such as "Nuevo día," written almost thirty years after the youthful *Don de la ebriedad*, demonstrates the relative stability of Rodríguez's poetic thought, with all of its internal contradictions. His poetry has undergone stylistic changes throughout the years, and each successive book has introduced new thematic concerns. In light of the great sophistication shown by the poems written at the beginning of his career, however, it would not be accurate to see these developments as fundamental changes. Especially dangerous are notions such as "maturity," which imply "immaturity" in the poet's early work. In this re-

spect it is significant that the later Rodríguez is consciously
reworking his own previous texts. In Rodríguez's late poetry, as in
his earliest poems, the poet searches for the exceptional moments of vision that arise from the capacity of language to negate
nonlinguistic reality. At the same time, he is aware that the
transcendent powers of language are inseparable from its duplicitous nature. He struggles to reconcile or to fuse the opposing
impulses that have defined his poetics from the beginning.

My treatment of Rodríguez's poetic works has been diachronic.
I have told a story of the development and refinement of a theory
of poetic language, considering each of his four volumes in the
order in which they were written and published. I have traced
the emergence of the ideal of participation from the visionary
poetics of *Don de la ebriedad*, the subsequent crisis of the participatory ideal in *Conjuros*, and the development of a more self-
consciously alienated stance in *Alianza y condena*. Finally, I
have studied the paradoxical poetics of the later work, from
Alianza through *El vuelo de la celebración* and other subsequent
poems. My primary aim throughout, however, has been the syn-
chronic reconstruction of Claudio Rodríguez's poetic thought as
it is articulated in varying forms at every stage of his career. Given
the essential continuity and coherence of Rodríguez's poetry over
the years, his future work is likely to continue to explore the
contradictions of poetic vision in words that remain conscious of
their own paradoxical nature.

6
Modern Poetry and the Language of Criticism

Every criticism is a criticism of the work and of itself.
　　　　　　　　　　　　　　　　　　　　—Barthes

The central premise in my reading of the poetry of Claudio Rodríguez has been that his poetic thought forms a coherent whole. The vision of the sign in his later work tends toward a fusion of the two opposing impulses that have defined his poetics from the beginning. The poet remains as committed as ever to the union of language and reality, while becoming increasingly aware of the essentially arbitrary nature of the link between words and things. The conflict between these opposing but interdependent attitudes toward language is a constant in Rodríguez's work. In the earlier books, however, the two attitudes were often presented as though they were alternatives to each other. In *Don de la ebriedad* the poet attempts to sacrifice his knowledge of the arbitrariness of the sign. In *Conjuros*, similarly, he rejects the ideal of social integration in order to attain a more critical vision. Beginning with the poems of *Alianza y condena*, it becomes increasingly difficult to separate the impulse to merge with the world and the desire to remain conscious of language in all of its contradictions. This tendency culminates in *El vuelo de la celebración*, in which the poet strives to participate in the world through the poetic act, but without losing awareness of the duplicity of the sign. Taken together, Rodríguez's books of poetry form a single, sustained meditation on the possibilities of poetic language.

Any attempt to reduce Rodríguez's poetics to either of its two opposing impulses would be misleading, for its coherence lies, paradoxically, in its contradictions. One could claim that the poet is ultimately pessimistic about the possibility of uniting language with the world. At the same time it is the search for such a union that defines his thought: his doubts about the word

133

would be inexplicable without an original faith. In contrast to a naively Cratylist poet (if any exists), Rodríguez is intensely self-aware, but he seems equally distant from the chimerical poststructuralist writer who would strive to create a purely arbitrary and autonomous poetic language. As his work develops it moves progressively toward a fusion of these two opposing attitudes toward language. In his later poems it becomes increasingly difficult to consider either in isolation from the other.

Any attempt to categorize Rodríguez's thought in this way, then, neglects one of its central insights: the inseparability of the two theories of poetic language. My own emphasis on the poet's linguistic self-consciousness has inevitably highlighted the arbitrariness of the sign, for to be aware of language at all is to recognize its limitations. The "romantic" view, in contrast tends to abolish the mediation of language altogether. Sobejano, in a remark typical of this approach, affirms that "leyendo la poesía de Claudio Rodríguez se tiene la impresión de que siempre habla el alma" [reading the poetry of Claudio Rodríguez one has the impression that the soul is always speaking].[1] An exclusive emphasis on the poet's distrust of language, however, risks being as reductive as this apparently more "naive" view. Analyzing the poems of El vuelo de la celebración, Miller defines Rodríguez's "linguistic skepticism" in terms of its opposition to the "linguistic faith" of Jorge Guillén.[2] This contrast is based on the one that Guillén himself makes in Lenguaje y poesía between "lenguaje insuficiente" and "lenguaje suficiente." The mystic or romantic poet—San Juan de la Cruz or Gustavo Adolfo Bécquer—distrusts language as the imperfect translation of an original experience. A writer such as Gabriel Miró or Guillén himself has faith in the capacity of language to communicate meaning. Rodríguez, without a doubt, is familiar with Guillén's argument: he summarizes it in his interview with Federico Campbell, citing the examples of San Juan, Bécquer, and Miró.[3] Yet he does not identify his own attitude with either alternative. It is clear that he does not share Guillén's faith in language as a sufficient medium. At the same time, he does not conceive of poetry as an attempt to translate an original, prelinguistic experience or idea into words. He has repeatedly emphasized that poetry does not begin until the actual writing of the poems, that there can be no "poetic experience" prior to language.

In his rejection of the separation between experience and language Rodríguez, along with many of his contemporaries, clearly rejects the position of the social poets, who saw writing as the communication of a content defined a priori. For Rodríguez, the inspiration for the poem is not an idea to be expressed, nor an ineffable, prelinguistic state of reverie: poetry arises from a reflection on language and a deciphering of signs. His work nicely illustrates the paradox found in the theoretical essays of Maurice Blanchot—writing is a search for its own origin, but this origin only exists in writing itself: "Pour écrire il faut déjà écrire."[4] Miller is correct when she asserts that "The coincidence between words and a purely objective reality is always partial for Rodríguez, and cognition therefore always incomplete."[5] Yet Rodríguez is rarely concerned with the positivistic idea of objectivity in the first place. When the poet insists upon the limits of language he does not, as Miller claims, exalt "the world beyond human subjectivity and language . . . the purely physical universe that is mute."[6] Rather, he attempts to create another language, a more authentically human speech. The world of nature, far from being inhuman and mute, is a web of signs that the poet interprets through the linguistic signs of poetry.

If poetic experience is the experience of language itself, then Guillén's distinction between sufficient and insufficient language loses much of its pertinence. In "La hermenéutica y la cortedad del decir," Valente argues that that topos of ineffability, or the incapacity of language to capture experience, is linked to the idea that poetic language is charged with meaning that is not apparent at the literal level: "¿No se convertiría, visto a esta luz, el tópico de la inefabilidad en tópico de la eficacia radical del decir? En efecto, la cortedad del decir, la sobrecarga de sentido del significante es lo que hace . . . que quede en él alojado lo indecible o lo no explícitamente dicho" [Viewed in this light, would not the topos of ineffability become the topos of the radical efficacy of speech? In effect, the surcharge of meaning of the signifier is what makes it contain the unsayable or that which is not explicitly said].[7] In other words, there is always more meaning within language than language itself can express. It is only through what it does not say that poetic language is able to suggest the experience of what cannot be said.

The paradoxical efficacy of "insufficient" language allows one to see the contrast between Guillén and the poets of Rodríguez's and Valente's generation in a somewhat different light. Miller concludes her article with the question of whether Rodríguez's "negative" view of language might be a self-fulfilling prophecy, in contrast to the confidence that permits Guillén to communicate more effectively with his readers: "Guillén's position of faith seems indeed to promote the communication he seeks, while in a sense Rodríguez's skepticism seems to impede it."[8] Yet the way in which this opposition is framed already assumes that poetry is primarily the communication of a given message, a view that Rodríguez would vigorously contest. To view the subversion of communication as evidence of a predominately negative attitude toward language is an oversimplification, for the very arbitrariness that alienates language from reality also allows it to transcend this reality. Only a poet with a deep commitment to the word would interrogate it so intensely. Miller herself notes that Rodríguez's view is more "balanced" than that of other modern writers who condemn language. Yet balance is hardly the word for Rodríguez's deep ambivalence toward the irreconcilable visions of the sign that govern his poetics. As the poet himself has succinctly put it: "O las amas demasiado [las palabras] o las odias demasiado" [You either love words too much or hate them too much].[9] The ambivalent attitude toward language evident in Rodríguez's work is also a defining characteristic of twentieth-century poetry. In this respect, the most significant contrast to be made is not between two different classes of poets, those who trust and those who distrust language, but between opposing visions of the sign within the work of individual poets. Guillén's faith in the word appears to be relatively uncomplicated, even naive, in comparison to Rodríguez's more modern position. A more complete view of Guillén's poetics, nevertheless, would have to take into account the dialectic between mimesis and autonomy within his theory of literary language. Guillén would probably not subscribe to the straightforwardly mimetic theory that "words are at our service in the faithful capturing of a given reality."[10] It would be more accurate to affirm that, for the author of *Cántico,* it is language itself that creates the reality of the poem. In his essay on Gabriel Miró, Guillén notes that the Levantine writer views experience as incomplete without language. Poetry is not the mere translation of a previously experienced reality into language but the completion or fulfillment of this experience: "No es sólo que la contemplación pueda encontrar su expresión adecuada. Miró dice más: el acto contemplativo se realiza del todo gracias al acto verbal" [It is not merely that contemplation is able to find its adequate expression. Miró says more: the contemplative act is completely realized through the verbal act].[11] Guillén, then, sees language as an addition to reality rather than a one-to-one representation of it. (Rodríguez might view it as a simultaneous addition *and* subtraction.) In this quite different way, Guillén, like Rodríguez, also recognizes the gap between language and reality. The important point is that neither poet would take the view that poetry is a mere copy of a previously defined reality.

Rodríguez himself, significantly, has recognized the need for a more sophisticated rereading of Guillén's work, one that over-turns the critical commonplace that attributes to him an uncom-plicated faith in language and in life: "Se ha escrito tanto de 'la poesía de la claridad' o del 'Ser' en *Cántico*, de una plenitud de situación y de realización, que parece anular y rechazar cual-quier ceguera o duda ante la posible oscuridad de la luz, ante una posible noche del claro día guilleniano" [So much has been written about the "poetry of clarity" or of "Being" in *Cántico,* of a plenitude of situation and of realization, that it seems to rule out or reject any blindness or doubt concerning the possible obscurity of the light, a possible night of the bright Guillenian day].[12] In a strikingly similar comment, Valente is even more definite, suggesting that the real poetic value of Guillén's work lies exclusively in these exceptional moments of doubt: "¿No habría que buscar, acaso por vía única, el residuo poético de *Cantico* en sus 'claroscuros,' en las brechas que otro tiempo o poder más real abre, a pesar de todo, en su ajustada geometría?" [Is it not necessary to seek, perhaps exclusively, the poetic resi-due of *Cántico* in its "chiaroscuros," in the gaps that another more real time or power opens, in spite of everything, in its adjusted geometry?][13] In their attempt to recuperate his work, these younger poets offer readings that appear to go against the grain of Guillén's own thought (although Guillén himself has acknowledged the "claroscuros" of *Cántico*). Rodríguez and Val-ente are, in effect, searching for the darker moments of Guillén's work that prefigure their own questioning of language and repre-sentation.

Any attempt to define the basic attitude toward language that characterizes modern poetry involves a circular argument, for *modern poetry* itself is defined by a particular linguistic vision, a self-reflexive exploration of the contradictions of poetic lan-guage. The definition of the *postmodern,* for similar reasons, is even more problematical. It would be easy to see the contrast between Guillén and the poets of Rodríguez's generation as an instance of the more general division in twentieth-century liter-ature between modernism and postmodernism.[14] In one view of modern literature, which is now widespread among critics, mod-ernism, characterized by a "rage for order," dominates the first

years of the century. Postmodernism, a movement toward inde-
terminancy, begins approximately with the literature published
after the second world war, and comes to fruition in the 1960s.
Yet the majority of the characteristics that have been attributed to
postmodernism—linguistic play, self-reflexiveness, indeterminacy, historical self-consciousness, the writerly text—are already present in the literature of the prewar period, especially in
avant-garde movements such as dada and futurism. To say that
such early phenomena are *exceptional* is to beg the question of
the definition of modernism. Part of the distortion stems from a
vision of the movement that is based almost exclusively on an
Anglo-American model. The proto-typical modernists of this
tradition include William Butler Yeats, the James Joyce of *Portrait
of the Artist*, T. S. Eliot, Virginia Woolf, and Wallace Stevens. The
common critical image is of an essentially conservative movement that emphasized the power of the individual artist to impose an ordered vision on the chaos of modern life. Although
Guillén's work would fall within this definition of modernism,
he is not necessarily typical of his period. The works of Pedro
Salinas, Vicente Aleixandre, Federico García Lorca, and Luis
Cernuda provide other, more self-reflexive models of modern
Spanish poetry. The Peruvian César Vallejo and the Chilean
Pablo Neruda also diverge from the Anglo-American definition of
modernism.[15] In general terms, modern Hispanic poetry has
more in common with the French avant-garde tradition that
stems from Lautréamont and Arthur Rimbaud.[16]

Viewed as clusters of traits rather than as discrete periods, both
modern and *postmodern* have increasingly been applied to literature of the past. Postmoderen literature is not limited to the
postwar period, nor modern poetry to poets of the late nine-
teenth century and after: the same conflict between opposing
visions of the sign underlies both baroque and romantic poetry.
Since both visions are inherent in poetic language, it could be
argued that the tension between them is present in virtually all
poetry. A postmodern poet would be one who reveals a consciousness of this tension. Once again, however, the definition is
circular, for the distinction between the implicit self-
reflexiveness of all poetry and the explicit self-commentary of
modern poetry is difficult to sustain. The suggestions that
Rodríguez and Valente offer for reading (or misreading) Guillén
reveal the possibility that postmodernity is not so much the
attribute of particular texts as it is a mode of interpretation. If a
modern text is one that reflects upon itself, a postmodern reading

is one that recognizes that all literature is self-reflexive. Such a reading, by revealing the latent self-awareness of an apparently "naive" text, would ultimately dissolve the distinctions between modern, postmodern and premodern poetry.

My explication of Rodríguez's poetry is situated ambiguously between a reconstruction of his system of poetics and the imposition of another system, derived from structuralism and semiotics, on his work. The source of this ambiguity lies in Rodrígeuz's peculiar status as a postmodern poet, at once obsessively conscious of the problems of poetic language and distant from the language of contemporary criticism. In this respect Rodríguez differs markedly from Valente, who has often adopted ideas from modern critical theory in order to define his own poetics. Rodríguez's statements about his own work often appear to be those of a traditionalist. My aim has been to elucidate Rodríguez's meditation on the poetic sign through another set of terms, one that he himself would not use when speaking of his own work. If, as Roland Barthes has suggested, the critical act is a game involving the interplay between two different systems of signs,[17] the distance between my critical commentary and Rodríguez's poetic self-exegesis is a potentially fruitful one. When faced with the task of explicating a poet who puts forward an explicitly self-conscious theory of literature, the critic often merely paraphrases this theory, echoing the poet's own reflections. The allegorical mode of Rodríguez's thought, the indirection of his meditation on the sign, allow for a more productive dialectic between the language of poetry and the language of criticism.

The self-consciousness of modern poetry adds a further complication to the interaction between the critic's and the poet's enterprise. Barthes analyzes critcism in terms of "the relation of the critical language to the language of the author studied, and the relation of this language object to the world. It is the 'friction' of these two languages which defines criticism . . ."[18] Yet the poet's words form not only a "language object," in Barthes's terms, but a "metalanguage" as well. The poet in Rodríguez's work is not only a creator but also a reader of signs, one who envisions the world itself as a text and who reflects upon the interrelation between his own language and these signs of the world. From this perspective, criticism, poetry, and reality form a chain of semiotic systems, each of which is a metalanguage interpreting the next:

critical language   →   poetic language
poetic language   →   the world as text
the world as text   →   the meaning of reality

The relation between each of these pairs is analogous. In each case the idea that there is a natural correspondence between the metalanguage and its object comes into conflict with the opposing idea that the relation between them is essentially arbitrary.

The symmetry between critical and poetic language implies that the game of criticism, in this case at least, is a reduplication of the structure of the poet's work. The critic of Rodríguez's poetry, like the poet-protagonist within the text, is faced with the contradictions of two opposing visions of the sign. Like the poet's interpretation of the world, the critic's reading involves a dialectic of distance and participation. Too close an identification with the poet's language would result in a loss of critical distance. An excessive distance, on the other hand, would transform criticism into a completely arbitrary imposition of one language onto another.

The use of a critical or theoretical metalanguage often produces the illusion of a greater lucidity: it appears to give its user a privileged vantage point from which to study literature. Much structuralist theory has sought to distance itself from the business of interpretation. An analogy to linguistics suggests the idea that the task of the poetician is to explain *how* literature signifies rather than to interpret individual works: the linguist, after all, studies the general functioning of language, not the meaning of individual utterances. This analogy, however, is inexact: while the linguist and the native speaker of a language are engaged in quite distinct activities, the theorist and the critic (as well as the writer and the reader) are united in a common interrogation of the literary sign. The act of interpreting the work of a self-conscious modern poet such as Claudio Rodríguez is a fundamentally theoretical enterprise. The theorist, by the same token, cannot reflect upon the process of reading without also taking part in this process.

The inseparability of literary criticism and literary theory is especially crucial to the study of the self-consciousness of modern poetry. It is here that the two senses of the term *poetics*—as the systematic theory of literature and as the consciousness of language implicit in the poet's work—come together. Poetics is no longer only a science of literature, to be studied from a detached, Olympian point of view, but also literature's consciousness of itself. Seen from this perspective, literary theory forms part of the larger exploration of language carried out by modern literature as a whole. It is only through rigorous readings of writers who struggle with the problems of the literary sign that we can come to understand the semiotic adventure of the literature of our time.

In the context of Spanish poetry, the generational group that includes Claudio Rodríguez, José Angel Valente, Angel González, Jaime Gil de Biedma, and Francisco Brines represents a major renewal of the linguistic self-consciousness that defines the work of modern poets from Mallarmé and Rimbaud on. Thus these poets have brought Spanish poetry back to the central current of modern and postmodern literature after its apparent rupture with this tradition during the civil war. In the view of many readers Claudio Rodríguez occupies a preeminent place among these poets. As I have attempted to make manifest in this study, the depth and rigor of his poetry and poetics make him one of the great poets of the twentieth century.

Notes

PREFACE

1. Quoted in Federico Campbell, *Infame turba* (Barcelona: Lumen, 1971), p. 239. All translations are mine, unless otherwise noted.
2. Ibid., p. 229.

CHAPTER 1. THE LANGUAGE OF POETIC VISION

1. Roland Barthes, *Critical Essays,* trans. Richard Howard (Evanston, Ill.: Northwestern University Press, 1972), pp. 97–98.
2. For a discussion of the issues surrounding the terms *modernism* and *postmodernism,* see the concluding chapter of this book.
3. Roland Barthes, *New Critical Essays,* trans. Richard Howard (New York: Hill and Wang, 1980), p. 68.
4. Gerald Bruns, *Modern Poetry and the Idea of Language: A Critical and Historical Study* (New Haven: Yale University Press, 1974), p. 1.
5. Jacqueline Vaught Brogan, *Stevens and Simile: A Theory of Language* (Princeton: Princeton University Press, 1986).
6. Dionisio Cañas. *Poesía y percepción (Francisco Brines, Claudio Rodríguez, José Angel Valente)* (Madrid: Hiperión, 1984); José Luis Cano, "La poesía de Claudio Rodríguez de Conjuros a *Alianza y condena,*" in *Poesía española contemporánea; generaciones de posguerra* (Madrid: Guadarrama, 1974), pp. 153–64.
7. Martha LaFollette Miller, "Claudio Rodríguez's Linguistic Skepticism: A Counterpart to Jorge Guillén's Linguistic Faith," *Anales de la Literatura Española Contemporánea* 6 (1981): 105–21.
8. Andrew Debicki, "Claudio Rodríguez: Language Codes and Their Effects," *Poetry of Discovery: The Spanish Generation of 1956–1971* (Lexington: The University Press of Kentucky, 1982), pp. 40–58, and Margaret Persin, "The Syntax of Assertion in the Poetry of Claudio Rodríguez," *Recent Spanish Poetry and the Role of the Reader* (Lewisburg, Pa.: Bucknell University Press, 1987), pp. 68–97.
9. I am aware that the two oppositions—"Orphic" versus hermetic poets, and the "Cratylist" motivation of the sign versus the arbitrariness of language—are not identical in all respects. The first opposition refers to more general poetic attitudes, whereas the second is more technical. In poetics, however, technical issues of semiotics often take on particular values.
10. Gérard Genette, "Valéry and the Poetics of Language," in *Textual Strategies: Perspectives in Post-Structuralist Criticism,* ed. Josué V. Harari (Ithaca: Cornell University Press, 1979), p. 373.
11. E. L. Epstein, "The Self-Reflective Artefact: The Function of Mimesis in

an Approach to a Theory of Value in Literature," in *Style and Structure in Literature: Essays in the New Stylistics*, ed. Roger Fowler (Ithaca: Cornell University Press, 1975), pp. 40–78.

12. Barthes, *New Critical Essays*, p. 68.

13. Tzvetan Todorov, *Theories of the Symbol*, trans. Catherine Porter (Ithaca: Cornell University Press, 1982), pp. 255–70.

14. Genette, "Valéry and the Poetics of Language," p. 361.

15. Barthes, *Critical Essays*, p. 275.

16. Gérard Genette, *Mimologiques: Voyage en Cratylie* (Paris: Editions de Seuil, 1976), p. 307. In my view Genette underestimates the degree to which these two positions are both contradictory and interdependent. He tends to privilege the motivation of the sign at the expense of the autonomy of literary language: "Grattez le formaliste, vous trouvez le symboliste . . . grattez Hermogène, vous (re)trouvez Cratyle" (p. 312). Todorov shares this bias toward motivation. He believes that Genette exaggerates the importance of the paradox in Jakobson's work that I regard as crucial, *Theories of the Symbol*, p. 280. Both theorists contrast Cratylism to the rationalistic theory of the conventional sign (Saussure), rather than to the richer semiotic tradition that takes language to be a deceptive veil concealing the truth or an autonomous system of signs that liberates itself from the world.

17. A critic approaching the problem from another theoretical perspective might claim that poetic language represents a fusion of these opposing impulses. While I would agree that poetry often reflects the struggle for such a reconciliation, I would still view the ultimate attainment of this state as a fiction.

18. Octavio Paz, *Corriente alterna* (Mexico: Siglo Veintiuno, 1967), p. 8.

19. John Deely, ed. *Frontiers in Semiotics* (Bloomington: Indiana University Press, 1986), p. xi.

20. Roland Barthes, *Writing Degree Zero*, trans. Annette Lavers and Colin Smith (Boston: Beacon Press, 1970), p. 15. The similarity between Barthes's position in this book and the young Spanish poets' objections to the often propagandistic verse of their elders is striking. See especially "Political Modes of Writing," pp. 19–28, and "Writing and Revolution," pp. 67–73. The French critic and Rodríguez's group are equally at odds with the aesthetics of socialist realism. Curiously, Barthes excludes poetry from his discussion of the morality of writing ("Is There Any Poetic Writing?" pp. 41–52).

Dionisio Cañas (*Poesía y percepción*, p. 141) precedes me in identifying the presence of an "ética de la escritura" in the work of these poets. For general discussions of Rodríguez's "generation," which includes José Angel Valente, Francisco Brines, Jaime Gil de Biedma, Angel González, Carlos Sahagún, Eladio Cabañero, and a few others, see Andrew P. Debicki, *Poetry of Discovery* (Lexington: The University Press of Kentucky, 1982), pp. 1–19, José Olivio Jiménez, *Diez años de poesía española: 1960–1970* (Madrid: Insula, 1972), pp. 15–32.

21. José Angel Valente, *Las palabras de la tribu* (Barcelona: Siglo XXI, 1971), p. 11.

22. Claudio Rodríguez, "Unas notas sobre poesía" in *Poesía última*, ed. Francisco Ribes (Madrid: Taurus, 1963), p. 90.

23. Umberto Eco, *A Theory of Semiotics* (Bloomington: Indiana University Press, 1976), p. 9; original emphasis.

24. Rodríguez, "Unas notas sobre poesía," p. 90.

Chapter 2. The Crisis of Visionary Poetics in Don de LA EBRIEDAD

1. *Corriente alterna*, p. 108.

2. According to Martha LaFollette Miller, the poems of *Don* demonstrate "la imposibilidad de hacer que el lenguaje coincida con lo que se pretende nombrar" [the impossibility of making language coincide with that which it attempts to name], "Elementos metapoéticos -en un poema de Claudio Rodríguez, "*Explicación de Textos Literarios* 8(1979–80):134." Whereas Miller's emphasis falls on the *frustration* of mimesis or of referentiality (she does not distinguish between the two), I take the distance between language and reality to be the point of departure for Rodríguez's meditation on the sign rather than its final destination. The poet is conscious of the duplicity of language from the very beginning. The question is whether this duplicity is primarily a means of questioning appearances or, on the contrary, an obstacle to his participation in the natural world.

3. I obtained my information concerning the order of the poems from a conversation with the poet on 16 March 1985. The first poems written, by and large, are those of "Libro tercero," the third of three sections, more "irrational" and difficult than the later poems in "Libro primero." "Canto del despertar," in "Libro segundo," is one of the earliest, whereas the other poem in the section, "Canto del caminar," is the last. In the first edition of *Don* the three "books" are simply assigned roman numerals.

Rodríguez admitted to me that the order of the poems as they appear in the book is somewhat arbitrary, as he did not know at the time how to arrange a book of poems as a coherent whole. Vicente Aleixandre shares in the responsibility for the arrangement of the next two collections of poetry, *Conjuros* and *Alianza y condena*.

4. All citations from *Don* will be taken from *Desde mis poemas* (Madrid: Cátedra, 1981), his latest collected works. Numbers in parentheses refer to book, poem, and page respectively. All translations of Rodríguez's poetry and commentary are my own, and are as literal as possible. The division into lines in the translation has a purely informative function: no specifically prosodic effect is intended.

5. Kenneth Burke, *Language as Symbolic Action* (Berkeley: University of California Press, 1966), p. 430.

6. Ibid., pp. 453–54; original emphasis.

7. Joaquín González Muela, *La nueva poesía española* (Madrid: Ediciones Alcalá, 1973), p. 59.

8. Enrico Mario Santí, in his discussion of Neruda's *Residencia en la tierra*, sees the poet's alienation as an essential feature of this mode: "In visionary poetry the revelation of an object's truth stems from the perception of an alienated subject," *Pablo Neruda: The Poetics of Prophecy* (Ithaca: Cornell University Press, 1982), p. 24.

9. Martha LaFollette Miller, analyzing this poem in her "Elementos metapoéticos," emphasizes the indeterminant nature of the night/day ambiguity: the reader cannot decide whether these lines refer to the sunset or the sunrise (pp. 129–30). In my opinion Miller overstates her case somewhat by interpreting the poem in isolation, neglecting the patterns of imagery of the sequence as a whole. The image of the night "closing the great chamber of its shadows," for instance, could *possibly* refer to dawn rather than nightfall, as she argues, but a

reading of the other poems in *Don* limits the meaning of the image: dawn is invariably depicted as the *opening* of the shadows, night as their closing.

10. Cañas, *Poesía y percepción*, p. 140.

11. González Muela calls this poem "pathetic" because it shows the inability of the poet to find concrete objects for his vision like Jorge Guillén's "concrete marvels." He links this shortcoming to Rodríguez's inexperience as a poet: "En este libro primerizo, él intenta ver, penetrar, adaptar bien su mirada; pero se queda insatisfecho y dudoso" [in this first book, he tries to see, to penetrate, to adapt his gaze adequately; but he remains unsatisfied and doubtful.] González Muela, *La nueva poesía española*, pp. 63–4. I would not view the "failure" of vision in such negative terms.

12. Stanley Fish, *Self-Consuming Artifacts: The Experience of Seventeenth-Century Literature* (Berkeley: University of California Press, 1972), p. 157.

13. Theories of reading tend to emphasize either the imposition of the self onto the text or else the text's manipulation of the reader. In his close readings of seventeenth-century texts, Fish shows how they lead the reader to question his or her own self. In his theoretical appendix to *Self-Consuming Artifacts*, and in subsequent discussions of reading, he claims that it is the reader who transforms the text rather than vice versa.

14. Cano, *La poesía española contemporánea*, p. 154.

15. Rodríguez, *Desde mis poemas*, 14. As the prologue continues, the author resorts more and more to direct quotation from his own poetry. He will quote some lines in their original verse format and then quote other fragments of poems in prose without acknowledging their source. He lifts whole passages from his own previous prose statements as well. The entire prologue is essentially a weaving together of other texts, both his own and others'.

16. Jonathan Culler, "Beyond Interpretation," *The Pursuit of Signs; Semiotics, Literature, Deconstruction* (Ithaca: Cornell University Press, 1981), pp. 3–17. Culler resolves this conflict by favoring literary theory over "new interpretations of literary works." A potential weakness in this position is that it leads to a reliance on secondhand readings. The semiotician takes the meaning(s) of the work as "given" and attempts merely to explain the system of codes and conventions that produces it. A text such as *Don*, which reflects upon the process of its own interpretation, makes it difficult to maintain this distance: the literary theorist, like the critic, is drawn into the poet's interpretive crisis.

17. Fish, *Self-Consuming Artifacts*, p. 410.

18. The distinction that Fish draws between *interpretation* and *reading* is useful, so long as one term is not privileged over the other. As a theorist (in *Self-Consuming Artifacts*), Fish insists on the priority (in both the temporal and logical senses of the word) of reading. As a critic, what he describes is the constant interplay, the dialectic, of these two aspects of a single process.

19. Miller, "Elementos metapoéticos." This poststructuralist interpretation oversimplifies *Don* at the opposite pole from Cano's romantic projections. She assimilates Rodríguez's poems rather hastily into a paradigm of reading that is common in literary criticism. The reader begins with the expectation of finding a representation of reality. Since the text resists this "naturalization," the reader is forced to interpret it as a metapoetic commentary on the failure of its own language. This paradigm would produce almost identical readings of any number of modern poets.

20. Kenneth Burke has distinguished between two types of literary form, which are analogous to the "symphony" and the "tone poem": "The symphonic

form contained a 'way in,' 'way through' and 'way out.' It sought to place a spell of danger upon us and in the assertion of its finale to release us from this spell. But the tone poem sought *to lead us in and leave us there.*" *The Philosophy of Literary Form,* 3rd ed. (Berkeley: University of California Press, 1973), p. 119; original emphasis.

21. Burke has studied the reversibility of logic and narrative in *A Grammar of Motives* (New York: Prentice Hall, 1945), pp. 430–40, and *The Rhetoric of Religion* (Berkeley: The University of California Press, 1961), pp. 222–36. Roland Barthes sees the basis of narrative itself as "the confusion of consecution and consequence, what comes *after* being read in the narrative as what is *caused by;* in which case narrative would be the systematic application of the fallacy denounced by scholasticism as *post hoc, ergo hoc* . . ." Barthes, *Image–Music–Text.* trans. Stephen Heath. (New York: Hill and Wang, 1977), p. 94.

CHAPTER 3. THE MOTIVE FOR METAPHOR

1. Santiago Daydí-Tolson, *The Postwar Spanish Social Poets* (Boston: Twayne, 1983), pp. 47–48.

2. Ibid., p. 68.

3. Claudio Rodríguez, "Unas notas sobre poesía," in *Poesía última,* ed. Francisco Ribes (Madrid: Taurus, 1963), p. 89.

4. José Luis Cano celebrates the work as an example of the pastoral, but without examining the artificiality of this genre. Critics usually date the beginning of Rodríguez's poetic maturity at *Alianza y condena* (1965), his third book of poetry. For these critics *Don de la ebriedad* and *Conjuros* represent, in contrast, a more innocent, unreflexive stage in his development. See, for example, Carlos Bousoño, "La poesía de Claudio Rodríguex," in Claudio Rodríguez, *Poesía 1953–1966* (Barcelona: Plaza y Janés, 1971), p. 31.

5. Kenneth Burke's remarks on rhetorical identification are pertinent here: "Identification is affirmed with earnestness precisely because there is division. Identification is compensatory to division. If men were not apart from one another, there would be no need for the rhetorician to proclaim their unity. If men were wholly and truly of one substance, absolute communication would be of man's very essence." *A Rhetoric of Motives* (New York: Prentice Hall, 1953), p. 22.

6. *Desde mis poemas,* p. 69. Subsequent references to this edition will be incorporated into the text.

7. Vicente Aleixandre, *Historia del corazón* (Madrid: Espasa-Calpe, 1954), p. 58. On the image of the public square in postwar poetry see Daydí-Tolson, *The Post-Spanish Civil War Social Poets,* pp. 143–49.

8. Philip Silver, in his analysis of "A una pared de adobe," reaches a similar conclusion. The poet calls upon the adobe wall to return to its condition as earth. Of all human activity, only the tilling of the soil does not do violence to nature: ". . . es una especie de intervención en beneficio de la tierra, y no sólo del ser humano" [It is a kind of intervention that benefits the earth and not only the human being]. "Claudio Rodríguez y la mirada sin dueño" in Claudio Rodríguez, *Antología poética* (Madrid: Alianza, 1981), p. 18.

9. In a passage from the introduction to *Desde mis poemas,* written many years after *Conjuros,* Rodríguez uses lameness as a metaphor for the alienation based on the mediation of language: "Gran parte de la poesía contemporánea

... queda coja, inválida ... por la distancia esencial del lenguaje ante las cosas" (p. 16).

10. William Empson, *Some Versions of the Pastoral* (London: Chatto and Windus, 1935), p. 15. Empson's view of proletarian literature as a "version of the pastoral" is especially relevant to Rodríguez's attempt to join the theme of social solidarity and the celebration of rural life.

11. Barthes, *New Critical Essays*, pp. 48–49.

12. Bousoño, "La poesía de Claudio Rodríguez," pp. 9–35.

13. Debicki, "Claudio Rodríguez, pp. 40–58.

14. Silver, "La mirada sin dueño," p. 12.

15. Mary Gaylord Randel has studied a similar ambiguity in the figurative language of the *Soledades*. There are two opposing yet complementary approaches to Góngora's metaphor: one can emphasize its allegorical meaning, in essence translating it into more familiar terms, or else value it as an autonomous display of virtuosity that overcomes the referentiality of language: "Metaphor and Fable in Góngora's *Soledad primera*," *Revista Hispánica Moderna* 40 (1978–79): 97–112.

16. Culler, *The Pursuit of Signs*, pp. 201–2.

17. This pattern is also frequent in the poems of Arthur Rimbaud, one of Rodríguez's favorite poets. See, for example, "Le bateau ivre," in *Oeuvres Poétiques* (Paris: Garnier Flammarion, 1964), pp. 88–91.

18. I quote these lines from the first edition of *Conjuros* (Torrelavega: Ediciones Cantalapiedra, 1958), p. 62. In later reprintings of this poem the last line reads "¡Ya por tan poco! Un grajo aquí, ya en tierra" [Failing by so little! A jackdaw here, already on the earth], muting if not completely eliminating the effect I am noting. A critical edition of Rodríguez's poems noting such revisions would be useful.

19. Roland Barthes, *S/Z*, trans. Richard Miller (New York: Hill and Wang, 1974), p. 20.

20. Debicki, "Claudio Rodríguez," pp. 44–45.

21. My sense of the development of *Conjuros* as a coherent book owes something to Michael Mudrovic, "The Progression of Distance in Claudio Rodríguez's *Conjuros*," *Hipania* 63 (May 1980): 328–34. According to Mudrovic, the first poems in the book represent a naive "rose-colored vision," with little distance between the speaker of the poem and the reality observed. As the work progresses Rodríguez employs increasingly disjunctive techniques to convey an increasingly disillusioned and insightful vision. While Murdrovic emphasizes the unity of the work, he does not consider many of the more obvious connections between the poems, such as repeated patterns of imagery and thematic development. He does not consider the poet's ambivalent status within his community or the question of social solidarity. Thus his conclusions remain excessively vague.

22. Silver, "La mirada sin dueño," p. 17.

CHAPTER 4. ALIANZA Y CONDENA

1. I am employing the term "dialectic" in the sense given by Kenneth Burke: "the employment of the possibilities of linguistic transformation." *A Grammar of Motives*, p. 402. Other relevant definitions might include: "the discovery of truth by the give and take of converse and redefinition ... the processes of interaction between the verbal and the non-verbal ... the internal dialogue of

thought . . . the placement of one thought or thing in terms of its opposite . . . the progressive or successive development and reconciliation of opposites." Ibid., p. 403.

2. In interpreting *Alianza* as a unified collection of poetry I have followed the approximate order in which the poems appear in the book. As with *Conjuros*, it was Vicente Aleixandre rather than Rodríguez himself who arranged the poems in book form. This arrangement, then, should not necessarily be taken as the last word.

3. The theme of the political corruption of language, of course, is a frequent one in the literature of nations governed by totalitarian regimes, ones that suppress the truth through censorship and deceit.

4. Gustav Siebenmann, *Los estilos poéticos en España desde 1900* (Madrid: Gredos, 1973), p. 409.

5. Rodríguez, *Desde mis poemas*, 134. Subsequent references to this edition will be incorporated into the main body of the text.

6. José Angel Valente, *Punto cero (Poesía 1953–1979)* (Barcelona: Seix Barral, 1980), p. 63.

7. In a rather transparent maneuver, the "Novísmos" have emphasized their own originality by treating all poets of value that preceded them in the postwar period as "exceptions" to what they view as the generally dismal situation of Spanish poetry of the time. In Rodríguez's generation, however, these "exceptions" clearly outweigh the "norm."

8. Several critics have studied Valente's metapoetry. See Jiménez, *Diez años de poesía española*; and Persin, *Recent Spanish Poetry and the Role of the Reader*. Some of these same critics, however, have ignored or even denied this aspect of Rodríguez's art. Olivio Jiménez, for example, treats the poet's search for the truth in purely thematic terms. "Hacia la verdad en *Alianza y condena* (1965), de Claudio Rodríguez," pp. 145–74. Persin claims that "Rodríguez does not give himself over to metapoetic reflection in his verse; his texts are not overtly self-conscious." *Recent Spanish Poetry*, p. 91. This surprising assertion is belied by the critic's post-structuralist approach, which leads her to examine the ways in which "Rodríguez's texts embody the difficulty of making language coincide with something exterior to it, in this case the enigmatic reality of ordinary experience." Ibid.

9. In order to argue his thesis that "Brujas" exemplifies "the rejection of a materialistic outlook on life," Mudrovic ignores the second half of the poem, assuming that the first roman-numbered section is a complete work in its own right: ". . . the first poem of the volume, 'Brujas a mediodía, I' . . ." "Claudio Rodríguez's *Alianza y condena*: Technique, Unity, Development," *Symposium* 33 (Fall 1979): 249. Nowhere does the critic attempt to justify this act of critical amputation, which in my opinion produces a misleadingly simple reading of one of Rodríguez's most complex poems.

10. Persin studies the use of rhetorical questions, along with other forms of equivocating syntax such as negation, antithesis, and the subjunctive mood. See especially her analysis of "Brujas a mediodía," *Recent Spanish Poetry*, pp. 83–91.

11. Siebenmann, *Los estilos poéticos*, p. 465.

12. Another poem that explores the ambiguity of the sign is "Dinero" (*Desde mis poemas* p. 158), a witty exploration of the idea of exchanging words for money, one kind of duplicitous sign for another.

13. Siebenmann, in a fine analysis of this poem, points out that the notion of

the gesture is a metaphor of all forms of human communication. *Los estilos poéticos*, pp. 463–66. Nevertheless, he stops short of considering the poem as metapoetry of a more explicit variety.

14. Quoted in Campbell, *Infame turba*, p. 229. The notion of the poem as a creative act of exploration underlies the poetics of Rodríguez's entire cohort. The title of Debicki's book, *Poetry of Discovery*, refers to this aspect of these poets' work. *Discovery* in this case translates *conocimiento*: "coming to know," a key word for Rodríguez, Valente, and their group.

15. Persin, for example, speaks of his "intuitive rather than logical approach toward language." *Recent Spanish Poetry*, p. 91. Such statements, which can be supported by some of the poet's statements about his own work, are misleading in that they underestimate the systematic coherence of Rodríguez's meditation on the sign. This coherence, of course, is not necessarily the result of a conscious intention on the part of the poet.

16. Mudrovic, "Claudio Rodríguez's *Alianza y condena*," p. 254.

17. The idea of the transcendent transformation of seemingly ordinary reality is one of the commonplaces of Rodríguez criticism. See, for example, Debicki, *Poetry of Discovery*; and Carole Bradford, "Transcendent Reality in the Poetry of Claudio Rodríguez," *Journal of Spanish Studies: Twentieth Century* 7 (1979): 133–46. None of these critics, however, has seen this phenomenon in specifically semiotic terms, as an interpretation of the signs of the world.

18. A more accurate translation of *condena* might be "sentence," as in a "prison sentence." I prefer "condemnation" as a word that has less restricted connotations in English.

19. Cano, "La poesía de Claudio Rodríguez," p. 158.

20. It must be remembered that the poets of Rodríguez's generation were children during the Spanish civil war. Any nostalgia that they might feel for their childhood is always tempered by the knowledge of the national tragedy that was occurring at the time. In Jaime Gil de Biedma's "Intento formular mi experiencia de la guerra" [I try to formulate my experience of the war], for example, the child's naive happiness—"Fueron, posiblemente, / los años más felices de mi vida" [They were possibly / the happiest years of my life]—contrasts with the adult poet's awareness of the war: "Mis ideas de la guerra cambiaron / después, mucho después / de que hubiera empezado la postguerra" [My ideas about the war changed / after, long after / the postwar had begun]. Jaime Gil de Biedma, *Las personas del verbo* (Barcelona: Seix Barral, 1982), pp. 122–24.

21. Quoted in Campbell, *Infame turba*, p. 231.

CHAPTER 5. THE LANGUAGE OF PARADOX AND THE PARADOX OF LANGUAGE

1. In a conversation with the poet (15 March 1985), I outlined the conflict between opposing impulses that I view as the basis of his poetics. He concurred with my theory but emphasized the difficulty of considering these two impulses in isolation from each other.

2. Pere Gimferrer, "Prólogo" to Vicente Aleixandre, *Antología total* (Barcelona: Seix Barral, 1975), p. 32.

3. Quoted in Campbell, *Infame turba*, p. 232.

4. Gonzalo Sobejano, "Impulso lírico y epifanía en la Obra de Claudio

Rodríguez," in *De los romances-villancicos a la poesía de Claudio Rodríguez,* ed. José Manuel López de Abiada and Augusta López Bernasocchi (José Esteban, 1984), p. 410–11.

5. Ibid., p. 413.

6. Nancy Mandlove, "Carnal Knowledge: Claudio Rodríguez and *El Vuelo de la celebración,*" *American Hispanist* 4, no. 32–33 (1979): 23.

7. Alan Bruflat, "Ambivalence and Reader Response in the Poetry of Claudio Rodríguez," Ph.D. diss., University of Kansas, 1986, p. 122.

8. See chapter 2. Bruflat presents an opposing view: "Strangely, the reader remains isolated from much of the process at work in *Don de la ebriedad.*" "Ambivalence and Reader Response," p. 39. My own view is that any such definition of "the reader" is an attempt on the part of the critic to impose a particular perspective on his or her own readers.

9. The combination of *con* and *sin* in Rodríguez's poetry offers multiple possibilities for ambiguity. In a copy of "Calle sin nombre" containing the poet's handwritten corrections, Rodríguez has changed "sin rutina, / sin uso" [without routine, with use] to "con rutina, / sin uso" [with routine, without use], thus making two words that were virtually synonymous into polar opposites. Other corrections to this poem give further insight into Rodríguez's creative process, which tends to work through the dialectical manipulation of oppositions. The last lines of the poems originally read:

> Tú no andes más. Di adiós.
> Tú deja que esta calle
> siga hablando por ti, aunque nunca vuelvas.
> ("Calle sin nombre," *Jarazmín, cuadernos de poesía* (Málaga) 9 (1982–83).

> Do not walk any more. Say goodbye.
> Let this street
> continue speaking for you, although you never return.

The revised version is quite different:

> Tú no andes más. Di adiós.
> Tú deja que esta calle
> ya nunca hable por ti, aunque siempre vuelvas.
> (Ibid.)

> Do not walk any more. Say goodbye.
> Do not let this street
> talk any longer for you, although you always return.

Rodríguez has revised, not in order to refine his expression of an idea, but to state the exact opposite, although the paradox of the line remains intact.

10. The opposition between "insufficient" and "sufficient language" that forms the basis of Guillén's argument is, in my view, an oversimplification. Poets who complain about the limits of language do so as part of an effort to break these limits and create a new kind of language. It is therefore misleading to claim that they have less faith in the word than those poets who celebrate the expressive power of language as it already exists. See chapter 6 for further discussion of these issues.

11. Carlos Bousoño has studied the modernity of San Juan's visionary lan-

guage. See *Teoría de la expresión lírica* (Madrid: Gredos, 1971), pp. 280–302. Luce López-Baralt, in a more recent work, traces the mystic poet's strikingly modern conception of poetic language to the traditions of Sufi mysticism: *San Juan de la Cruz y el Islam* (Mexico, D.F.: El colegio de México, 1985). Another Spanish poet of Rodríguez's generation who shares his interest in the connections between mysticism and modern poetics is José Angel Valente. See his "La hermenéutica y la cortedad del decir," *Las palabras de la tribu* (Madrid: Siglo XXI, 1971), pp. 59–70, and "Rudimentos de destrucción," Ibid., pp. 71–74.

12. Burke, *The Rhetoric of Religion*, pp. 1–42.

13. Luce López-Baralt, typically, states that San Juan "ha terminado por vencer al lenguaje con el lenguaje mismo" [has ended up conquering language with language itself]. *San Juan de la Cruz y el Isalm*, p. 84. What she sees as his victory *over* language, however, could equally be said to be a victory *of* language. Paradox and polysemia are only destructive if one conceives of language as a predominately rational and denotative system of signs.

14. One could search for the "referent," on the other hand, in the poetic system of *El vuelo de la celebración*. There are numerous references to "dolor," and "herida" in the book. One of the central themes of Rodríguez's later poetry is the process of grieving. (I am indebted to Michael Predmore for this observation.)

15. One could also interpret these lines as "this accurate deception of the gaze, *after it has been transfigured into something else* by your transparence, gives me confidence and repentance." In this case the transparence of the tear would be a remedy for the "engaño" rather than its cause. This would invert the normal notion that the medium distorts the message: the normally deceitful signs ("la mirada") would be purified by the authenticity of the medium.

16. Bruflat employs this phrase in his chapter "*El vuelo de la celebración:* Free Play and Consolidation," pp. 102–139.

17. The comparison and opposition between the act of speech and the kiss is frequent in the poetry of Vicente Aleixandre, especially in his *Poemas de la consumación*.

18. At this writing Rodríguez is reportedly preparing another collection of poems, entitled *Casi una leyenda* (Almost a Legend), for publication.

19. Anthologized in José Luis García Martín, *Poesía española 1982–1983: Crítica y antología* (Madrid: Hiperión, 1983), pp. 178–79.

20. García Martín, *Poesía española 1982–1983*, p. 69.

21. See chapter 2 for a detailed discussion of this poem.

22. Rimbaud, *Oeuvres poétiques*, p. 139.

23. Philip Silver has also noted the double meaning of the word "originality," which has been often applied in a very loose sense to Rodríguez's poetry: *La casa de Anteo: Estudios de poética hispánica (De Antonio Machado a Claudio Rodríuez)* (Madrid: Taurus, 1985), pp. 220–21. Another similar word is "radical," which implies both a destruction of tradition and a return to roots.

Chapter 6. Modern Poetry and the Language of Criticism

1. Sobejano, "Impulso lírico y epifanía en la obra de Claudio Rodríguez," p. 409.

2. Miller, "Claudio Rodríguez's Linguistic Skepticism," 105–21.

3. Quoted in the interview with the poet in Campbell, *Infame turba*, p. 239.

4. Maurice Blanchot, *L'éspace littéraire* (Paris: Gallimard, 1955), p. 234.

5. Miller, "Linguistic Skepticism," p. 116.

6. Ibid., p. 107.

7. Valente, *Las palabras de la tribu*, pp. 67–68.

8. Miller, "Linguistic Skepticism," p. 118.

9. Quoted in Campbell, *Infame turba*, p. 239.

10. Miller, "Linguistic Skepticism," p. 117.

11. Jorge Guillén, *Lenguaje y poesía* (Madrid: Alianza, 1969), p. 146.

12. Claudio Rodríguez, "Unas notas sobre la poesía de Jorge Guillén," *Insula* 435–36: 7.

13. Valente, *Las palabras de la tribu*, p. 116.

14. I am indebted to Andrew P. Debicki for suggesting the relevance of postmodernism to the poets of Rodríguez's generation.

15. A relevant study of Neruda's poetry is Enrico Mario Santí, *Pablo Neruda: The Poetics of Prophecy* (Ithaca: Cornell University Press, 1982).

16. It is no coincidence that an important critic of contemporary American poetry has seen Rimbaud as the founder of the "other tradition" of modern poetry. See Marjorie Perloff, *The Poetics of Indeterminacy: Rimbaud to Cage* (Princeton: Princeton University Press, 1981). Perloff avoids the chronological problem by seeing modern literature in terms of two traditions: the symbolist tradition of determinate meaning, which she traces back to Mallarmé, and the poetics of indeterminacy, with its roots in Rimbaud. I depart from this view somewhat, for these two attitudes toward meaning are often in conflict in the work of a single author, including Mallarmé himself.

17. Barthes, *Critical Essays*, p. 258.

18. Ibid.

Bibliography

WORKS BY CLAUDIO RODRíGUEZ

Don de la ebriedad. Madrid: Ediciones Rialp, 1953.

Conjuros. Torrelavega: Ediciones Cantalapiedra, 1958.

Alianza y condena. Madrid: Revista de Occidente, 1965.

Poesía, 1953–1966. Barcelona: Plaza y Janés, 1971.

El vuelo de la celebración. Madrid: Visor, 1976.

Antología poética. Edited by Philip Silver. Madrid: Alianza, 1981.

Desde mis poemas. Madrid: Cátedra, 1981.

"Unas notas sobre poesía." In *Poesía última*, edited by Francisco Ribes, pp. 87–92. Madrid: Taurus, 1963.

"Calle sin nombre." *Jarazmín, cuadernos de poesía* (Málaga) 9 (1982–83).

"Nuevo día." In *Poesía española 1982–1982: Crítica y antología*, edited by José Luis García Martín, pp. 178–79. Madrid: Hiperión, 1983.

"Unas notas sobre la poesía de Jorge Guillén. *Insula* 435–36 (1983): 7–8.

"Claudio Rodríguez o la influencia de todo" [interview]. In *Infame Turba*, by Federico Campbell, pp. 228–40. Barcelona: Lumen, 1971.

WORKS ABOUT CLAUDIO RODRíGUEZ, AND OTHER WORKS CITED IN THE TEXT

Aleixandre, Vicente. *Historia del corazón*. Madrid: Espasa-Calpe, 1954.

Barthes, Roland. *Critical Essays*. Translated by Richard Howard. Evanston, Ill.: Northwestern University Press, 1972.

——. *Elements of Semiology. Writing Degree Zero*. Translated by Annette Lavers and Colin Smth. Boston: Beacon Press, 1970.

——. *Image–Music–Text*. Translated by Stephen Heath. New York: Hill and Wang, 1977.

——. *New Critical Essays*. Translated by Richard Howard. New York: Hill and Wang, 1986.

——. *S/Z*. Translated by Richard Miller. New York: Hill and Wang, 1974.

Bousoño, Carlos. "La poesía de Claudio Rodríguez." In *Poesía 1953–1966*, by Claudio Rodríguez, pp. 9–35. Barcelona: Plaza y Janés, 1971.

——. *La poesía de Vicente Aleixandre: imagen, estilo, mundo poético*. Madrid: Insula, 1950.

Bradford, Carole A. "Francisco Brines and Claudio Rodríguez: Two Recent Approaches to Poetic Creation." *Crítica Hispánica* 2 (1980): 29–40.

153

————. "From Vicente Aleixandre to Claudio Rodríguez: Love as a Return to the Cosmos." *Hispanic Journal* 4 (Fall 1982): 97–103.

————. *Teoría de la expresión lírica*. 5th ed. Madrid: Gredos, 1971.

Brogan, Jacqueline Vaught. *Stevens and Simile: A Theory of Language*. Princeton: Princeton University Press, 1986.

Bruflat, Alan Scott. "Ambivalence and Reader Response in the Poetry of Claudio Rodríguez." Ph.D. diss., University of Kansas, 1986.

Bruns, Gerald. *Modern Poetry and the Idea of Language: A Critical and Historical Study*. New Haven: Yale University Press, 1974.

Burke, Kenneth. *A Grammar of Motives*. New York: Prentice-Hall, 1945.

————. *Language as Symbolic Action*. Berkeley: University of California Press, 1966.

————. *The Philosophy of Literary Form*. 3d ed. Berkeley: University of California Press, 1973.

————. *A Rhetoric of Motives*. New York: Prentice-Hall, 1953.

————. *The Rhetoric of Religion: Studies in Logology*. Berkeley: University of California Press, 1970.

Cañas, Dionisio. *Poesía y percepción (Francisco Brines, Claudio Rodríguez, José Angel Valente)*. Madrid: Hiperión, 1984.

Cano, José Luis. "La poesía de Claudio Rodríguez de *Conjuros* a *Alianza y condena*." In *Poesía española contemporánea: generaciones de posguerra*, 153–64. Madrid: Guadarrama, 1974.

————. Review of *El vuelo de la celebración*, by Claudio Rodríguez. *Insula* 359 (October, 1976.): 8.

Culler, Jonathan. *The Pursuit of Signs: Semiotics, Literature, Deconstruction*. Ithaca: Cornell University Press, 1981.

————. *Structuralist Poetics: Structuralism, Linguistics, and the Study of Literature*. Ithaca: Cornell University Press, 1975.

Daydí-Tolson, Santiago. *The Post-War Spanish Social Poets*. Boston: Twayne, 1983.

Debicki, Andrew P. "Claudio Rodríguez: Language Codes and Their Effects." In *Poetry of Discovery: The Spanish Generation of 1956–1971*, 40–58. Lexington: The University Press of Kentucky, 1982.

Deeley, John, Brooke Williams, and Felicia Kruse, eds. *Frontiers in Semiotics*. Bloomington: Indiana University Press, 1986.

Díaz-Plaja, Guillermo. "Poesía de Claudio Rodríguez." In *Al pie de la poesía*, 188–192. Madrid: Editora Nacional, 1974.

Eco, Umberto. *A Theory of Semiotics*. Bloomington: Indiana University Press, 1976.

Empson, William. *Some Versions of the Pastoral*. London: Chatto & Windus, 1935.

Epstein, E. L. "The Self-Reflective Artefact: The Function of Mimesis in an Approach to a Theory of Value in Literature." In *Style and Structure in Literature: Essays in the New Stylistics*, edited by Roger Fowler, 40–78. Ithaca: Cornell University Press, 1975.

Fish, Stanley E. *Self-Consuming Artifacts: The Experience of Seventeenth-Century Literature*. Berkeley: University of California Press, 1972.

Garciasol, Ramón de. Review of *Don de la ebriedad*. *Insula* 99 (March 1954): 7.

Genette, Gérard. *Mimologiques: Voyage en Cratylie*. Paris: Editions de Seuil, 1976.

———. "Valéry and the Poetics of Language." In *Textual Strategies: Perspectives in Post-Structuralist Criticism*, edited by Josué V. Harari, 359–73. Ithaca: Cornell University Press, 1979.

Gil de Biedma, Jaime. *Las personas del verbo*. Barcelona: Seix Barral, 1982.

Gimferrer, Pere. "La poesía de Claudio Rodríguez." *Triunfo* (July 1970).

Guillén, Jorge. *Lenguaje y poesía*. Madrid: Alianza, 1969.

González Muela, Joaquín. *La nueva poesía española*, 59–80. Madrid: Ediciones Alcalá, 1973.

Jiménez, José Olivio. "Claudio Rodríguez entre la luz y el canto: sobre *El vuelo de la celebración*." *Papeles de sons Armadans* 87 (1977): 103–24.

———. "Hacia la verdad en *Alianza y condena* (1965) de Claudio Rodríguez." In *Diez años de poesía española, 1960–1970*, 145–74. Madrid: Insula, 1972.

López-Baralt, Luce. *San Juan de la Cruz y el Islam*. México, D. F.: El Colegio de México, 1985.

López Castro, Armando. "La mirada natural de Claudio Rodríguez." *Hora de Poesía* 45 (May–June 1986): 5–32.

Mandlove, Nancy. "Carnal Knowledge: Claudio Rodríguez and *El vuelo de la celebración*." *American Hispanist*, 4, no. 32–33 (1979): 20–23.

Miller, Martha LaFolette. "Claudio Rodríguez's Linguistic Skepticism: A Counterpart to Jorge Guillén's Linguistic Faith." *Anales de la Literatura Española Contemporánea* 6 (1981): 105–21.

———. "Elementos metapoéticos en un poema de Claudio Rodríguez." *Explicación de Textos Literarios* 8 (1979–80): 127–36.

Molero, Juan Carlos. "La poesía de Claudio Rodríguez." *Levante*, Valencia, 1966.

Mudrovic, William Michael. "Claudio Rodríguez's *Alianza y condena*: Technique, Development and Unity." *Symposium* 33 (Fall 1979): 248–62.

———. "The Poetry of Claudio Rodríguez: Technique and Structure." Ph.D. diss., University of Kansas, 1976.

———. "The Progression of Distance in Claudio Rodríguez's *Conjuros*." *Hispania* 63 (May 1980): 328–34.

———. "Time and Reality in Claudio Rodríguez's *El vuelo de la celebración*." *Anales de la literatura española contemporánea* 6 (1982): 123–40.

Núñez. Antonio. "Encuentro con Claudio Rodríguez." *Insula* 234 (1966): 4.

Octavio Paz. *Corriente alterna*. Mexico: Siglo Veintiuno, 1967.

Perloff, Marjorie. *The Poetics of Indeterminacy: Rimbaud to Cage*. Princeton: Princeton University Press, 1981.

Persin, Margaret. "The Syntax of Assertion in the Poetry of Claudio Rodríguez." In *Recent Spanish Poetry and the Role of the Reader*, 68–97. Lewisburg, Pa.: Bucknell University Press, 1987.

Prieto de Paula, Angel L. "Claudio Rodríguez entre la iluminación y la muerte." *Insula* 444–45 (November–December 1983): 7–8.

Randel, Mary Gaylord. "Metaphor and Fabel in Góngora's *Soledad primera*." *Revista Hispánica Moderna* 40 (1978–79): 97–112.

Riffaterre, Michael. *Semiotics of Poetry*. Bloomington: University of Indiana Press, 1978.

Rimbaud, Arthur. *Oeuvres poétiques*. Paris: Garnier Flammarion, 1964.

Ruiz Barrionuevo, Carmen. "La poesía de Claudio Rodríguez a la vista de *El vuelo de la celebración*" *Alamo* 57 (1976): unpaginated.

Salas, José M. "Algunas notas sobre la poesía de Claudio Rodríguez." *Cuadernos Hispanoamericanos* 334 (1978): 125–41.

Santí, Enrico Mario. *Pablo Neruda: The Poetics of Prophecy*. Ithaca: Cornell University Press, 1982.

Sanz Echevarría, Alfonso. "*El vuelo de la celebración* de Claudio Rodríguez." *Jugar con el fuego: Poesía y Crítica* 2 (1976): 47–51.

Segovia, Tomás. "Retórica y sociedad: cuatro poetas españoles." In *Contracorrientes*, 275-98. México: Universidad Autónoma de México, 1973.

Siebenmann, Gustav. *Los estilos poéticos en España desde 1900*. Madrid: Gredos, 1973.

Siles, Jaime. "Dos versos de Claudio Rodríguez y una prosa de Pedro Salinas: ensayo de reconstrucción." *Insula* 444–45. (November–December 1983): 6–7.

Silver, Philip. "Claudio Rodríguez o la mirada sin dueño." In *Antología poética*, by Claudio Rodríguez, 7–21. Madrid: Alianza, 1981.

———. *La casa de Anteo: Ensayos de poética hispánica (De Antonio Machado a Claudio Rodríguez)*. Madrid: Taurus, 1985.

Sobejano, Gonzalo. " 'Espuma' de Claudio Rodríguez." *Consenso: Revista de literatura* 2, no. 3 (1978): 37–50.

———. "Impulso lírico y epifanía en la obra de Claudio Rodríguez." In *De los romances-villancico a la poesía de Claudio Rodríguez: 22 ensayos sobre las literaturas española e hispanoamericana en homenaje a Gustav Siebenmann*, edited by José Manuel Lopez de Abiada and Augusta López Bernasocchi. José Esteban, 1984.

Todorov, Tzvetan. *Theories of the Symbol*. Translated by Catherine Porter. Ithaca: Cornell University Press, 1982.

Valente, José Angel. "Ensayo sobre Miguel de Molinos." In *Miguel de Molinos: Guía espiritual*, edited by José Angel Valente. 11–51. Barcelona: Barral, 1974.

———. *Las palabras de la tribu*. Madrid: Siglo XXI de España Editores, 1971.

———. *Punto cero (Poesía 1953–1979)*. Barcelona: Seix Barral, 1980.

Vargas-Churchill, Alicia. "La coherencia de 'Espuma' de Claudio Rodríguez." *Explicación de Textos Literarios* 14 (1985–86): 25–34.

Villar, Arturo del. "El don de la claridad de Claudio Rodríguez." *Estafeta Literaria* 2, no. 3 (1976): 20–23.

Index

157

DATE DUE
